The Secret Oral Teachings in Tibetan Buddhist Sects

Alexandra David-Neel

and

Lama Yongden

*To the late Lama YONGDEN, my
adopted son and the faithful com-
panion of 40 years of adventurous
travels and study in the East, who
helped me to collect these informa-
tions in Tibet.*

THE LAMA YONDGEN

THE SECRET ORAL TEACHINGS
IN TIBETAN BUDDHIST SECTS

CHAPTER I

It is a long time since the idea of writing this book occurred to me. One fine summer afternoon I had explained my plan to a learned Tibetan who led a life of contemplation in a little house on the rocky side of a mountain. He was not encouraging.

"Waste of time," he said. "The great majority of readers and hearers are the same all over the world. I have no doubt that the people of your country are like those I have met in China and India, and these latter were just like Tibetans. If you speak to them of profound Truths they yawn, and, if they dare, they leave you, but if you tell them absurd fables they are all eyes and ears. They wish the doctrines preached to them, whether religious, philosophic, or social, to be agreeable, to be consistent with their conceptions, to satisfy their inclinations, in fact that they find themselves in them, and that they feel themselves approved by them."

The Master had nothing to teach me on this point. Hundreds of times, in the West, I had heard

men and women express the desire to find a religion
which would satisfy them, or had seen reject a
doctrine with the remark: "It does not satisfy me."

What, then, was that *something* that wanted to
be agreeably caressed, satisfied?—It was the collection
of false notions, of unreasonable propensities, of feelings of a rudimentary sensuality which is disguised
under the appearance of a puppet named "I". I
thought then of the devotees who intoxicate themselves with incense and the stirring sonorousness of
the organ in the half shadows of our cathedrals,
believing themselves to be on the way to spiritual
heights. I thought of all those, whatever might be
the religion or secular faith to which they belong,
who thrill at the sound of certain names, of certain
words which are but empty noises devoid of reality.

"In general," continued the Master, "we distinguish three kinds of individuals: those whose intelligence is completely dull; those whose intelligence is
of average quality, able to understand some Truths
which are specially evident; those endowed with an
intelligence better equipped for acute perceptions,
who are fit to penetrate below the surface of the world
of physical phenomena and grasp the causes which
are at work there.[1]

---

[1] These three degrees being called respectively: *thama, ding* and
rab . . . . written thama, hbring and rab.

"It is enough to direct the attention to these last, to say to them: 'Look from this point of view, consider that' and they perceive what is to be perceived there where they have been told to look; they understand what is really the thing which one has pointed out to them.

"One may proclaim on the high road the Teachings considered secret, they will remain 'secret' for the individuals with dull minds who will hear what is said to them, and will grasp nothing of it but the sound.

"It is not on the Master that the 'secret' depends but on the hearer. A Master can only be he who opens the door: it is for the disciple to be capable of seeing what lies beyond. Teachers exist who are able to discern the degree of intellectual acuteness of those who desire their Teaching, and they reserve the detailed explanation of certain doctrines for those whom they judge able to understand them. It is thus that the deep Teachings, transmitted orally from Master to disciple for many generations, have been passed on and preserved from oblivion. You have heard them. Do with them as you think fit. They are very simple, but, like a powerful battering-ram, they run counter to the wall of false ideas rooted in the mind of man and the emotions which delight him casting him into suffering . . . . . Try!"

Then, I remembered what the ancient Buddhist Texts tell us about the hesitation of the Buddha before beginning His Mission:

"I have discovered a profound Truth, difficult to perceive, difficult to understand, accessible only to the wise.

"Human beings busy themselves in the vortex of the world and find there their pleasure. It will be difficult for men to understand the law of the concatenation of causes and effects, the suppression of the samskāras[2]. . . .

"Of what use to reveal to men that which I have discovered at the price of laborious efforts? Why should I do so?—This doctrine cannot be understood by those filled by desire and hatred . . . . it is mysterious, deep; hidden from the vulgar mind. If I proclaim it and men are unable to understand it, the only result will be fatigue and annoyance for me."

"And as He thought thus, the Venerable One[3] felt inclined to remain quiet without preaching the Doctrine."

---

[2] The samskâras are the mental formations, the ideas, the conceptions that one forms, and which depend on ignorance. See below for a detailed explanation.

[3] *Bhagavan* is a respectful title used in speaking to religious personalities. The Sannyāsins (Hindu ascetics) use it among them-

At this point the Texts, with Oriental imagination, tell of the intervention of a God, Brahmā Sahampati, who put into words the thoughts springing up in the mind of the Buddha.

Brahmā Sahampati exhorts the Buddha to conquer His hesitation:

"May the Venerable One preach the Doctrine! There are beings whose spiritual eyes are hardly darkened by light dust, these will understand the Doctrine. In the land of Magadha[4] a false doctrine has prevailed up to the present, elaborated by men whose minds were contaminated (by ignorance). Now open to them the gate of Immortality (literally, of the deathless).

"Arise, O Victorious One! Travel throughout the world, O Chief of Pilgrims (beings who wander in the round of successive births and deaths). There are some who will understand Thee."

---

selves. This title is also given to certain Gods. *Bhagavan* means: glorious, illustrious, revered, etc. English writers have, in most cases, translated this word by "Blessed One". French writers have given an identical translation with "Le Bienheureux" which does not correspond to the real meaning of *Bhagavan*. "Venerable" is nearer to the meaning the Indians give to *Bhagavan* when they use this word.

[4] The ancient kingdom of Magadha in Central India, which was the scene of the Buddha's activities.

"Then the Buddha cast a supremely clair-voyant look over the world. He saw some beings whose spiritual eyes were hardly covered by thin dust. He saw some whose minds were keen and others whose minds were dull.

"Just as in a pond, among lotus flowers born in the water, some do not emerge from the water and bloom in the depths, others grow to the sur-face of the water, and others emerge from the water and the water does not wet their flowers, so the Buddha, casting His eyes on the world saw some beings whose minds were pure from the filth of the world, beings with keen minds and others with dull minds, beings of noble character, good listeners and bad. When He had seen these things he spoke to Brahmā Sahampati, saying:

"Let the Gate of the Eternal be open to all! Let him who has ears to hear, hear!"

I doubt whether the divine Brahmā Sahampati judged me worthy of his intervention. Nevertheless, I have ventured to apply to myself the advice which he once gave to the Great Sage of India, and depending also on the permission which was given me on the threshold of a Tibetan hermitage, I shall attempt to summarise this collection of theories and precepts named "sangwa", the secret mystical doctrine, closely bound up with the idea of *lhang tong*[5] transcendent insight.

The teachings of all the Masters who left nothing written and even those of the numerous Masters whose authentic works we possess have always given rise to interpretation, to developments which, in some cases, have added to and brought out the significance of the original doctrine, and in others have falsified the initial meaning.

I have said elsewhere[6] that an account of the Buddhist Doctrine can be given on two pages, and I have, in fact, given in tabular form covering two pages, the fundamental Teaching of Buddhism. All schools of Buddhism, without exception, accept them and take them as the basis of what they consider legitimate developments and interpretations of them.

To discuss this legitimacy is not always easy. The Buddha insisted strongly on the necessity of examining the propositions put forward by Him, and of understanding them personally before accepting them as true.

The ancient texts leave no doubt on this point:

"Do not believe on the strength of traditions

---

[5] Spelt respectively in Tibetan: gsang wa and lhag mthong.

[6] In "Buddhism, Its Doctrines and Methods"—John Lane, the Bodley Head, London. French edition 'Collection du Rocher—Plon, Paris. German edition Brockhaus, Wiesbaden.

even if they have been held in honour for many
generations and in many places ; do not believe
anything because many people speak of it ; do
not believe on the strength of sages of old times ;
do not believe that which you have yourselves
imagined, thinking that a god has inspired you.
Believe nothing which depends only on the authority of your masters or of priests. After investigation, believe that which you have yourselves tested
and found reasonable, and which is for your good
and that of others."[7]

Elsewhere, after conversing with some of His
disciples, the Buddha concluded :

"If, now, you understand thus, and see thus.
will you say : We honour the Master and it is
out of respect for Him that we speak thus?"

"We shall not do so."

"What you say, O disciples, is it not only that
which you have yourselves recognized, yourselves
understood?"

"It is exactly that, Venerable."

During the centuries subtle Indian and Chinese
philosophers have largely availed themselves of the
freedom of thought and interpretation which was

[7] Kālāma Sutta.

allowed them. They have used it with skill and we have profited by the stories of astonishing contests of polemics.

The Tibetans did not fail to imitate them, and one can recognize in their guarded oral teachings an interesting conjunction of Indian philosophy and the special mentality of the Yellow races. On the other hand, the best informed contemporary adepts of the Sect of Meditation (Dhyāna) called *Ts'an* in China and *Zen* in Japan, readily agree that their doctrine is Buddhism understood by the minds of the Yellow race.

This admixture of different mentalities has left in the Buddhism of secret teachings in Tibet a special quality of transcendent rationalism, a strict intellectual equilibrium which completely differentiates it from the popular religion as also from the emotional mysticism of certain Mahayanist schools.

It is evident that the great majority of those who call themselves Buddhists have not been able to rise to the mental level of the Teaching of the Buddha.

Most of them have built up for their own use various kinds of Buddhism which are anything but Buddhist and, in their ignorance, they uphold, often with bitterness, their belief and their absurd practices as the expression of the purest orthodoxy.

The more intelligent see clearly the illogicality of

these "varieties" of Buddhism, but they submit to them, accepting them as an indispensable concession made to the mental weakness of the "mass" and because they wish to group a "mass" of individuals under a label which does not suit them.

A very learned Japanese who shows a very special indulgence—may I say a tenderness—towards these degenerate forms of Buddhism, express himself thus:

"We may sometimes ignore the claims of reason and rest satisfied, though usually unconsciously, with assertions which are conflicting when critically examined, but we cannot disregard by any means those of the religious sentiment which finds satisfaction only in the very fact of things. If it ever harboured some flagrant contradiction in the name of faith it was because its ever pressing demands had to be met with even at the expense of reason."

Elsewhere the same author wrote:

"The inflexibility of karma is more than poor mortal can endure."[8]

_____

[8] Professor D. T. Suzuki in "Outlines of Mahayana Buddhism", pp. 218 and 283.

That is possible, that is probably true of most of those about us, but who compels these weak-minded people to call themselves Buddhists?—Is it not open to them to attach themselves to other doctrines which offer them tales apt to flatter their sentimental tendencies?—In so doing they need not fear any eternal damnation, but only the distressing momentary accidents which the mistakes they commit in their physical and mental activity, their deeds and thoughts, may bring upon them.

The Tibetan Masters who pass on the traditional oral teachings repeat insistently the fact that these teachings are for the use of individuals in the *rab* category, that is to say endowed with superior and excellent intelligence, the "lotus whose flowers grow above the level of the water" accordinig to the picturesque comparison quoted above.

The object of these teachings is not to amuse the simple-minded, those charitably called in the Tibetan Scriptures the "children", it is meant for the strong to make them stronger, for the intelligent to make them more intelligent, for the shrewd to develop their shrewdness and to lead them to the possession of transcendent insight (*lhag thong*) which constitutes the real enlightenment.

It is for such reasons that the explanation of the doctrines and methods which make up this corpus of teachings is reserved for certain class of disciples, and this fact has caused it to be called secret.

This Buddhism of a Tibetan elite is genuinely of Buddhist inspiration and dates from the most brilliant period of Buddhist philosophy. Its teachings are considered to be traditional having been handed down from Master to disciple in an uninterrupted line.

Those initiated in the secret teachings declare that these latter do not spring from a supernatural revelation but are the fruit of intellectual and spiritual investigations made by men who also combined with them investigations on the material plane.

On this point the advantage given to us by the data supplied by modern science is worth noting, an advantage helping us to understand the theories put forward by the Secret Teachings. The men who thought of these latter must have been endowed with superior faculties of understanding; they possessed transcendent insight: *lhag thong.*

Although the mythical personage Dorji Chang[9] is often named at the head of the list of those who transmitted the teachings, he is there in a symbolic sense insomuch as he is the "bearer of the magic sceptre", the *dorji* representing the power conferred

---

[9] Tibetan spelling: *rdor rdji htchang;* his Sanskrit name is Vajradhara: "He holds the Thunderbolt sceptre", like Zeus among the Greeks.

by the traditional teachings. Even if some people may be tempted to consider Dorji Chang as a real person, disseminator of special doctrines, none would venture to suggest that he was the author of such teachings.

The attainment of transcendent insight is the real object of the training advocated in the traditional Oral Teachings, which do not consist, as so many imagine, in *teaching* certain things to the pupil, in *revealing* to him certain secrets, but rather in showing him the means to learn them and discover them for himself.

The Masters of the secret teachings say that the truth learned from another is of no value, and that the only truth which is living and effective, which is of value, is the truth which we ourselves discover.

If this were not the case, it would be enough for us to read the innumerable works in which philosophers, savants and doctors of the different religions have explained their views and to choose from among them one which agrees with our own ideas and to which we can cleave. This is what is done by most of these individuals whom the Tibetans classify in the intermediate category of the average-minded.

This stage should be surmounted. It is not enough to see with eyes which, according to the words used in Buddhist Texts, "are only covered with a thin film of dust", however thin this film may be; it is a question of removing the last trace of dust which interferes with sight.

Literally, *lhag thong*, means to see "more", to see "beyond", to see "extremely", "supremely". Thus, not only to see more than that which is seen by the mass of mankind who are crassly ignorant, but to see beyond the bounds limiting the vision of cultivated minds, to bring into being the third eye of Knowledge which the adepts of tantric sects place in the centre of the forehead of their symbolic Gods.

CHAPTER II

The faith commended to their faithful by all religions, and considered by them as a virtue essential for him who hopes for eternal salvation, is nowise approved in the Secret Teachings. Based on the advice given by the Buddha to His disciples, the primary recommendation that the Masters give to neophytes is: "Doubt!"

Doubt is an incitement to research, and research is the Way which leads to Knowledge.

It does not follow from the above that he who undertakes to follow the Path of the Secret Teachings is thrown wholly on his own resources. By no means. He is put face to face with certain facts, facts which have always seemed to him so obvious that he has never given them a moment's thought, and the Master says to him: "Now investigate whether these facts which you accept as representing a reality are, truly, real. Examine them attentively and at length, putting aside all preconceived ideas, empty your mind of all the opinions which it has harboured concerning these facts ; *doubt* that which you have mechanically admitted up to the present, look as you would look at quite new things, those which form your physical environment; you will then investigate the mental reactions to which they give rise.

To examine the people among whom we find ourselves, to investigate the manifold phenomena which continually arise and disappear around us, and then to reach the point at which we examine the spectator of this spectacle, whom we call "I", that is truly an interesting programme which promises unforeseen discoveries.

To whom should we address our questions to obtain information about the world? From whom have we received that knowledge which we already possess?—

The reply is: from our senses.

We have seen, heard, tasted, smelt, touched various objects, either material or of a more tenuous nature. We have given names to these various objects, we have classified them in series of similar objects, we have built up, with them, a world which has become familiar to us in the same way as we furnish a house in which we live.

It is now a matter of shaking off the sluggishness created by the habit of busying ourselves without curiosity in *our* world, persuaded that the nature of its paraphernalia is perfectly known to us.

It is a matter of suspecting the information given us by our senses. Is this information true?—Do not we ourselves add, on our own authority, various accretions for which our senses are in no way responsible?

Let us see:

You happen to be in a vast, bare plain, and in the distance you see a fleck of green standing out on the yellow sand. What is the size of the fleck which you see?—Measure it in comparison with an upright object at eye-level, a ruler or even your finger. To what height on the ruler or on your finger does the green spot come?—Mark this height. It may be equal to the top joint of your little finger or even smaller ; it may be just a point.

If you have not already done it, you can, provisionally, stop at this very rudimentary experiment.

What have you *seen*?—You have seen a green spot of the size which you measured. You have seen that and nothing more. To say that you have seen a tree in the distance is incorrect. Your eyes did not show you a tree with leafy branches able to shelter you from the sun's rays. The idea of the tree and its representation in your mind are the results of mental activity which has been set in motion by the sight of the tiny fleck of green.

Many elements have been combined in this activity. One can put, in the first case, habit, memory. Other green spots seen in similar conditions have led to the finding of a tree at the end of a plain. This has been remembered. In a general way one knows also that distance gives a dwarfed image of objects seen, and this too has been remembered.

Nevertheless these are *ratiocinations* and not the fact of having *seen* a tree. It is *probable* that walking towards the green spot, he who saw it will find a tree, but this is not *certain*. The fleck of green may be found to be a building painted green, the green canvas of a tent, or something else which is not a tree. A higher degree of probability, if not certainty may be attained if, to the perception of the colour green, were to be added that of outlines suggesting the shape of a tree. But again, how many times will not the mental activity, applied to the sensation of seeing a green spot, go astray?—Dazzlement caused by the sun, mirages, can *cause us to see* not only green spots but trees and many other objects although these have no corresponding substance.

In short, what kind of information has been given to us by the fact of having seen a green spot?— It has simply made us conscious of having felt a sensation. A sensation, nothing more, all the rest is interpretation. In the same way, all our perceptions, those to which we give names and assign form, colour, or no matter what attributes, are nothing but interpretations of a fugitive contact by one of our senses with a stimulus.

Thus we are led to contemplate the co-existence of two worlds: that of pure contact not coloured by the screen of "memories", and that created by the mental formations (the samskāras): the interpretation.

The first of these worlds represents Reality, and is indescribable ; we cannot think anything, cannot imagine anything about it without "interpreting" and thus destroying its character of Reality. Reality is inexpressible and inconceivable.

The second of these worlds is that of mental formations set in motion by the contact-stimulus. It is the world in which we live. To say that it is not *real* does not mean that it is devoid *of existence*.[1]

*

* *

How is the phenomenal, tangible world represented in the Oral Secret Teachings?

The tangible world *is* movement, say the Masters, not a collection of moving objects, but movement itself. There are no objects "in movements", it is the movement which constitutes the objects which appear to us: they are nothing but movement.

---

[1] Tsong Khapa, founder of the Sect of Gelugspas (called Yellow Hats after the colour of their hat) insists on this point which puts him in opposition to the ultra-idealists represented nowadays by the Sect of the Dzogschen-pas.

This movement is a continued and infinitely rapid succession of flashes of energy (in Tibetan *tsal* or *shoug*). All objects perceptible to our senses, all phenomena of whatever kind and whatever aspect they may assume, are constituted by a rapid succession of instantaneous events.

Each of these momentary happenings is brought about by manifold causes and multiple conditions acting together. Here one should not think that the event is distinct from these causes and conditions. It is these which, together, constitute the event. Apart from them there is no event.

This word *event* must not be taken in the sense in which it is understood in ordinary language, that is to say as meaning a fact of exceptional importance as when one speaks of a "historical event". Event here means "something which happens". These "somethings" arising instantaneously and in series, these rapid flashes of energy are sufficiently like one another during the series to remain imperceptible to us, then suddenly occurs, in this series of moments, a different moment which catches our attention and makes us think that a new object has appeared.

This process is often explained by comparing it with the grain which remains apparently inert in the barn, then one day shows a germ, that is something differing from the grain. However, the inertness of

the grain of corn was only in appearance. That
which we saw as a lifeless grain was a series of combinations of causes and conditions, a series of separate
instants among which occurred other "instants" which
we saw as a germ.

Some people say that the germ is a transforma-
tion of the grain. The Secret Teachings do not seem
to encourage this opinion. The germ, they say,
exists *in dependence* on the grain according to the
classical Buddhist-formula: "This existing, that
arises" which is not to be understood as meaning that
this is the father who has begotten *that* by a transmission of substance. *This* is only the occasion which
rendered possible the appearance of *that*.

There are two theories and both consider the
world as movement. One states that the course of
this movement (which creates phenomena) is continuous, as the flow of a quiet river seems to us. The
other declares that the movement is intermittent and
advances by separate flashes of energy which follow
each other at such small intervals that these intervals
are almost non-existent.

As to the existence of matter which is motionless
and homogeneous, this is flatly denied.

*

* *

Although brief and incomplete, the summary which I have just sketched of the doctrines laid down in the Oral Teachings concerning the nature of the world, allows us to revert to the indications which our senses give us, tó examine them in greater detail.

When you look at an object, what happens?—A contact of the organ or sight with an exterior object. This contact lasts only for a flash. When you think that you are looking for a long time, what in fact happens is a series of repeated contacts, each one of which lasts only for an instant, and of which none is identical with the previous one.

Why not identical?

For several reasons, of which the principal one which includes all the others, is that—as has already been explained—nothing that exists is motionless, and that phenomena, whatever they may be, consist in a succession of changes following each other with a speed which is far beyond our faculties of perception and understanding.

Well then, the material organ called the eye which consists of an aggregate of a large number of cells[2] is not motionless. The cells which compose it are in perpetual movement; they are sensitive, indi-

---

[2] The expression "cell" is mine. A Tibetan would say *doul ten* (rdul phren) or *doul ta* (rdul phra), two terms corresponding also to molecule and atom, and also figuratively, to a grain of dust, and, in

vidually, to numerous influences brought to bear on them by agents exterior to them[3] and undergo numerous changes depending on the nature of their own evolution. The eye, at the moment of the second contact, is not identical with the eye which underwent the first contact, and it continues to change during the repeated contacts.

In fact, what these contacts have brought to us when we believed we "looked at length" is a series of images. The rapidity of the contacts caused us to see them as a single image.

In the same way, the object at which we were looking is itself not a homogeneous and motionless block. It is a "universe" formed by a large number of particles in movement. What has been said above of the cells which form the eye applies equally to those which constitute the object at which we have been looking. In their incessant dance they also undergo changes due to their own evolution and changes caused by exterior agents. Again, they move away from or near to each other, forming different arrangements,

---

any case, serving to express the idea of infinitely small particles which constitute the body. They translate the Sanskrit words: *anou* and *paramanou*.

[3] The word exterior should not be understood here as applying to agents existing outside the eye. The exterior agent may be for a cell, its neighbour more or less close, existing in the same aggregate, that is to say in the substance of the eye.

different patterns. It follows that the object envisaged changes, in reality, from one moment to another.

Although the majority of men are misled by the illusion which hides from them the forces at work both in the organ and in the object with which it is in contact, it does not follow that all men share the same error to the same degree.

"Transcendent insight", *lhag thong*, may come into play here. We can easily admit that our senses are very unreliable guides because they are not sufficiently acute ; we may even admit that they are wholly unsuited to allow us to perceive the ultimate basis of phenomena, but it is also reasonable to believe that our senses are susceptible to education and that their acuity can be increased. To what degree can this be done?—It is impossible to forsee it, but it is reasonable to suppose that we have by no means reached the limit of perception of which our physical and mental faculties are capable.

What has been said about the sense of sight and its object, naturally applies as well to other senses : the ear, a little universe in motion like the eye, and to its object, sound ; to odours and to the nose ; to taste and to the tongue ; to the sensations felt by the contact of our skin with a foreign body. In every case it is a question of the meeting of two aggregates in motion, and also, in every case, it is a matter of a sensation followed by an *interpretation* which brings it into the realm of consciousness while distorting it.

Can we propound the question: Among these multiple and intermingled contacts, which one gives us real knowledge?—We must beware of the word *real* which, when we use it, simply corresponds to an idea that we ourselves develop, to a manner of understanding which is peculiar to us or which we have adopted on the suggestion of others. In any case, no experimenting can put us in touch with Absolute Reality for it is with his senses that the experimenter perceives the progression of the experiment he carries out, and its results; now his senses, as has just been explained, only gives him various series of sensations which he interpretes in his own way. It is probable that this way of understanding is always very different from the reality.

But is there a Reality, a unique Reality in the absolute sense?—What can we know of it and what meaning would it have for us who do not belong to the world of the Absolute but to that of the relative?

Reality is synonymous with Existence. That which is real, that which exists, is that which produces effects. How, then, do we know that a thing produces effects?—We know it when we perceive them, when we feel the effects. Now each of us feels the sensations which the composition of his being allows him to feel;

A man neither feels nor perceives exactly as a mosquito or a plant does. A being other than human: a God, a Demon or no matter what other being, does not perceive as we do. The extent, the gradation, the strength, the nature of the sensations and the perceptions differ according to the constitution of the organ of contact of different beings. It follows therefore that that which is real, which exists, which produces effects for one, does not affect the other, has no reality, no existence for him.

Each sphere, each world, each order of beings possesses a Reality of its own because it produces effects in this special sphere and for this order of beings.

We must beware of ideas and judgments based on our human mentality, on our human senses and of relating and gauging according to our measure that which exists in the infinity of space.

*

*   *

One can very well apply to the Oral Teachings what has been said above concerning the discontinuity of the movement which *is* the world. This teaching is not expressed in a consequent and methodically arranged manner, as we might be tempted to wish. The subjects explained are interlaced, repeated, seen from various points of view. It is rare that a graduated "course" is given to a particular student. The teaching is composed rather of separate interviews often taking place at very long intervals. My observations consist in assembling the summaries of conversations I have heard. Each of my readers must connect together those of these summaries which are most interesting to him.

As I have stated at the beginning of this book, the method employed in the Oral Teachings is to suggest to the enquirer various subjects for reflexion and it is for him to make what he can of them. For some people the theories which they have touched will serve as a key to open the door to a field which until that moment, had been closed to them, while others will turn the key in their hands without putting it in the lock, or even will not suspect that there exists a door to open. This comparison is in accordance with the thought of the Masters who impart the Oral Teachings.

*

* *

Relying on the preceding explanations, I feel that I may return to the subject of contacts in order to develop it and insist on certain points.

It has been said that the contact of a sense with

its object is made up of a series of evanescent contacts.
It has also been stated that during these contacts both
the sense-organ and the object with which it is in
contact undergo changes because both are aggregates
of particles in movement.

The intensity of the different contacts varies.
Only some among them awake an echo in the mind,
this echo being translated into the idea which occurs
to us: "I have seen a horse",—"I have seen a tree, a
man".—"I have heard the gong being beaten"—"I
have eaten an apricot",—"I have smelt the odour of
burning wood",—"I have touched silken materials",—
"I have been pricked by a thorn", etc.

We see, hear, taste many things of which we are
not conscious and the lower an individual is in the
scale of physical and psychic development, the smaller
is the number of his conscious perceptions.

It is not a rare occurrence to have seen a landscape,
day after day, for a long time, and then suddenly to
pick out, in this familiar landscape, some object
which one had never seen, the sharp point of a *chörten*[1]
showing above a hill, or the mouth of a cave in a
rocky cliff. These things have always been there, our
gaze has rested on them many times, our organs of
sight have received an impression of them, but this
has not been strong enough *to make us see them*

---

[1] *Chörten,* a religious monument often seen in Tibet.

consciously. Other conditions having occurred, the impression has been strengthened and we have *seen*.

The competition of the senses among themselves also causes the temporary predominance of one or the other which smothers the sensations caused by the others.

An individual listening intently to a noise which concerns him, the galloping of horses which he thinks are ridden by brigands and coming towards him, will not feel the sting of insects, a cold wind, etc.

Does this mean that these contacts which fail to bring about enough mental activities to make us conscious of the kind of sensation felt, give rise to no effect of any kind?—By no means. Nothing which happens remains without effect.

Thus we are led to the examination of what can be these effects, that is to say what becomes of these numerous contacts of which we are not conscious.

We must add to the contacts due to the activity of our five senses those which result from the activity of our mind which is considered by Buddhists as the sixth sense. This last category includes the opinions, theories, doctrines, ideas in general which we have formed during our education, conversations which we have had or heard, reading which we have done, and so on. Among these contacts made by our sixth sense—the mind—as among those made by our physical senses, a large number, have lightly touched our mind without making a mark in it, or perhaps the impressions having been too faint, we have forgotten them.

However they are by no means dead for they have engendered descendants of a mysterious kind, and these descendants, that is to say, their effects, may manifest their existence even after a long interval.

Nevertheless we should not imagine that the forces set in motion by the physical or psychic contacts of which we have not been conscious, remain stored in a purely latent state in some kind of immaterial receptacle, awaiting conditions favourable for their manifestation.

Some people hold an opinion of this kind and speak of a "receptacle of consciousness" in a way which makes a sort of individual or cosmic deity of it. This opinion is contradicted in the Oral Teachings.

The forces caused by the contacts, both those of which we were conscious and those of which we were unwitting, give rise to manifold flashes of activity which are in evidence on different planes, and, at the same time, to multiple actions and reactions between these different forces themselves.

The interplay of the contacts and of their effects must not be envisaged in reference to ourselves alone.

The innumerable contacts of all kinds which continually occur in the universe and the equally innumerable and varied effects of these contacts, constitute another exchange of energy whose influence operates on all beings and in all spheres.

In order to follow the theories which we are examining more closely, it is better to say: "There are in reality no contacts happening in the universe. The universe *is* movement and this movement is made up of *contacts*. The contacts and their effects *are* the universe".

In the same way, on the restricted scale of our individuality, it is this movement of contacts and their effects which *is* our individuality, that which we call our "self".

Let us return once again to the facts within reach of this "self" which presently we shall see disappear like the "water of a mirage" or "the castle in the clouds".

The contact begets an idea. The birth of an idea may certainly depend on the contact, but nevertheless there is no certainty that the contact is the sole cause of the kind of idea which follows it.

We can compare the contact to a shock, but in the infinitesimal lapse of time between this shock and the arising of the idea which attaches a name to the object of the contact, a phenomenon happens.

This phenomenon may be compared to the inter-
position between the pure contact and our consciousness, of a screen on which figures are painted.

What is this screen?—The Tibetan calls it
pagtchags (in Sanskrit *vāsanā*) which means propen-
sity, inclination, habit, but more exactly: memory.[5]

The role played by education in the consciousness which arises from our perception has been
pointed out by western psychologists.

In an article on the way in which individuals
perceive colours, Dr. Charles Hill[6] expresses doubt as
to the exactitude of perception of a child who says the
grass is green. Has the child really the impression
that he sees the colour green when he looks at a lawn,
or does he repeat "the grass is green" as a result of
suggestion?—He has been told that "grass is green"
and so he sees it green.

In the as yet restricted field of research to which
the student is still limited, he will primarily examine
the habit which we have of associating the notions of
certain forms, certain colours, certain sounds, certain
tastes, with certain particular stimuli.

This habit is in no way personal. It is rooted,
from their beginning, in the beings whose organ of
contact are similar to our own and which therefore

---

[5] Another meaning of *vāsanā* is "force", "vital impulse".
[6] Article in the "Continental Daily Mail" of August, 1950.

are liable to be affected in the same way by the same stimuli. It is impossible for us to know the reactions of beings constituted in a different way. It is, however, reasonable to think that in the same world, as we have just said, different worlds are perceived by different beings according to the nature of their respective organs of perception.

The mechanism of the phenomenon may be summarised as follows: we know that when a contact takes place it consists of a series of intermittent contacts among which some produce a shock which gives rise to a sensation. This sensation has already been felt by the individual and by those of his species and the response made to it in analogous circumstances arises like a screen on which the habitual response to that kind of sensation is pictured in images: a horse, an apricot, a gong, a thorn or some other thing.

Does that mean that *in absolute truth* our senses have made contact with a real horse, a real apricot, etc.? There is no proof of this, for the only existing proof depends on the evidence of the senses, evidence which only repeats the inexactitudes formerly registered. We cannot presume any thing more than the existence of a stimulus which has caused the sensation that we have felt, a sensation which we have

interpreted in our own way, adding to it images of
our own invention.

Should we then believe that we have been taken
in by a pure mirage? Not entirely. Probably the
stimulus corresponds to something, but this something, that is to say the object[7] of some kind with
which one of our senses has made contact, remains
unknown to us.

Without any corresponding material object existing, we see in dreams images of horses, apricots, etc.
resulting from the memories we have of these objects.
In the following chapters we shall examine different
theories current on this subject.

*
*   *

The Tibetans did not fail to note that when
from a distance we see a hunter fire a shot we see
the flash before we hear the noise of the shot. This
observation, however, does not seem to have impelled
them to have followed up their investigations on this
subject and to work out any, more or less, coherent
theories about the respective velocities of light and
sound.

-----

[7] Here, we should not attach to the word "object" the idea of
materiality which it implies when we think of a stone, a tree or an
animal. In this content, the "object" is rather a force, a particular
flash of energy which our senses have met.

Nevertheless, the idea that the picture of the world which we behold really represents the condition of things happening at the moment when it appears to us, is plainly held to be doubtful in the Secret Teachings. These Teachings tend to believe that the images we see are images of *that which has been* and which *is no longer*. In other words that we see the images of dead things.

It may be interesting to compare, on this point, the data of our modern science with the conjectures found in the Secret Teachings.

Under the heading "If we were on a star, what would we see of that which exists on the earth?"— Alexander Ananoff, a distinguished member of the French Astronomical Society, wrote:

"On account of the enormous distances which separate us from the stars and the length of time which the light of a star takes to reach us, the image of the star which we see, is the image of this star which started out, several thousand years ago, from the point where the star was situated at the moment, and which is only now imposed on our retina.

"Thus we may conclude that, in most cases, it is the phantom of a star which we see. It is even possible that we are looking at a star which does not exist any longer, in which case we may think that to study astronomy is to study the history of a past which has disappeared.

"If we found ourselves on a star, and if, from there we could see the life on our planet, we should not see modern civilisation. We should for example see the events occurring in Egypt in the time of the Pharaohs."

To prove that the image of an object which we perceive is not exactly identical with that shown at the moment at which a conatct, visual or other, occurred, the Teachings point to the theories which deny any character of stability and solidity to material bodies. These theories have been briefly explained in the preceding pages.

Although the interval of time that they consider elapses between the moment when we perceive the image of an object and that at which the image of it "left", may be infinitely short, the principle involved is the same as that which relates to the thousands of years taken by the image of the star to reach us.

In both cases the conclusion is: "those things we see are images of the past".

The student is also told to think over the following problem: ought we to consider events as a series of pictures passing before a motionless spectator or ought we rather to believe that a traveller is marching along a picture gallery, contemplating, one after the other, the scenes represented by them.

This same problem is set to the Chinese of the Sect of Meditation,[8] and they seem to have found an answer to it in the following declaration which is famous in their Sect:

> "I am on the bridge, and O marvel! It is not the river which flows, it is the bridge which moves over the torrent."

The bridge which moves over a motionless torrent may be understood as the traveller walking past a succession of images which are the events, but preferably, it is the mind in continual motion which imagines the river (the torrent of events) flowing under the bridge, and which imagines the bridge itself.

Do these events already exist? Are they planted along the traveller's road like the motionless milestones which mark out our highways?

In this case would it suffice for the traveller to journey fast enough for him to contemplate the scenes which were out of eyeshot of these individuals who had either remained stationary or who were moving slowly, that is to say, for him to see that which is the

---

[8] Ts'an in China, Zen in Japan, Dhyāna in Sanskrit.

future for these individuals who were behind him on the road?

I have heard this traveller compared to a horseman. The faster his horse carries him, the sooner will he see such and such a river, a mountain and the people living in their neighbourhood which the slower foot-traveller will only see on the morrow or the day after.

On the other hand, would it be possible to go backwards, to retrace one's steps and then to contemplate scenes from the past?

On this point the Secret Teachings include various disconcerting statements such as that about the moving bridge and others like it. But, exactly like the Ts'an Masters, those who impart the Secret Teachings warn their pupils that these statements are in no way dogmatic. They aim at producing a mental shock, an upsetting of our habitual ideas which forces us to see an aspect of things which has never appeared to us and the possibility of the existence of the exact opposite of that which, up till then, we had considered as unassailable truth.

According to the picturesque expression of an adept of the Ts'an Sect, one must come "to see the Pole star in the southern hemisphere".

As to the possibility of having a vision of things to come, the point of view of the Secret Teachings is examined later.[9] Let us say at once that, based on the theories of the impermanence of phenomena, their instantaneousness and the multiplicity of causes on which they depend, these teachings state that the future cannot be seen except under the aspect of probabilities, never under that of certainty. The example given is often that of a seed from which *probably* a sprout will come, without however, there being any certainty of this, for it may dry out or, perhaps from some other cause, it may be that the seed will not produce any sprout.

The future like the past represents a relative conception which relates to an individual imagined as remaining motionless. It is relative to this individual supposed to be fixed to a definite spot and at a definite moment, that time and space exist. If I say *"distant"* my estimate really means *"distant from me"* or far from an object chosen by me and supposed, equally, to be fixed in a certain place.

It is the same if I say *"it is a long time"*, when the estimate of time is based on the fact of my existence, or on that of an object selected by me, and at a certain fixed moment.

What is meant by "it was a thousand years ago" or "yesterday"? What is meant by "near" or "at an

---

[9] In Chapter IV.

incalculable distance"? These terms mean nothing
in themselves ; far or near can only mean far from
or near to something, a thousand years or yesterday
can only be a thousand years or yesterday in relation
to something.

Is there any reason for lingering to discuss
problems of this kind?—The Masters who inculcate
the Secret Teachings do not think so. These discus-
sions, like other similar ones, may be useful as mental
gymnastics, useful to make the mind supple, but they
have no utility because the objects providing the
subject on which our mental cleverness is exercised,
have no real existence.

What has to be understood is that theories and
doctrines of all kinds are the fabrication of our mind.
It is capable of fabricating some of them diametri-
cally opposed to each other and one will be no truer
nor less true than the other because they are all
based on false perceptions or, at best, relative ones
which are only of value for an observer constituted
as we are, placed where we are, and such perceptions
have no absolute reality.

The celebrated philosopher Nāgārjuna[10] was a
past-master in the arts of baffling our mental habits,
of proving to us that the contrary to that which we

---

[10] The founder of the Madhyamika School of Philosophy. About
the second century C.E.

consider true could be equally true, and that, very often, both were absurd. In this fashion, he showed clearly the futility of our opinions which are inherited and upheld without even having examined the proofs on which they are said to be based.

CHAPTER III

The Buddhist Scriptures state that the first sermon of the Buddha consisted mainly of an explanation of the theory of the "Interdependent originations" (Pratitya samutpāda)[1] known also as the doctrine of the twelve causes.[2]

All the schools of philosophy which have developed in Buddhism, whether of realistic or of idealistic tendencies, have adhered to this. The philosopher Kamalasila[3] described the *pratitya samutpāda* as "the Jewel of the Buddhist Doctrine".

The Chain of "Interdependent Originations" is as follows:

---

[1] In Tibetan *rten hbrel yen lag btchu gnis*. Pronounced: *Ten del yen lag chu gni*. A good example of the difference which exists between spelling and pronunciation in the Tibetan language.

[2] The twelve *nidāna*.

[3] Kamalasila. A celebrated Buddhist philosopher of the sixth century. He belonged to the Monastery of Vikramasila in the land of Magadha (Central India). During the reign of King To tsong .detsen (Khri srong ldehu bstan), he went to Tibet and there competed in public controversy against a Chinese monk, an adept in the doctrine of non-activity. Kamalasila defeated his opponent and the latter was expelled from Tibet. In reading the story of this debate, in the Tibetan texts, it seemed to me that the arguments of the Chinese were superior to those of Kamalasila, but each time I suggested this to the Doctors of Philosophy of the Universities of Lhasa, they became angry . . . which did not alter my opinion.

	In Sanskrit	In Tibetan	
		Pronunciation	*Spelling*
Ignorance	avidya	marigpa	ma rig pa
Samskara (mental formation or compounds). ...	samskara	du che	hdu byed
Consciousness ...	Vijnana	namparshéspa	rnam par shés pa
Name and form (Body and Mind) ...	Nama—rupa	ming tang zug	ming tang gzugs
Sphere of the Senses (senses and their objects; the mind being counted as the sixth sense).	Sadayatana	kyé tchéd toug	skiémtchéd trug
Contact	sparsha	rég pa	régpa
Sensation ...	vedana	tsorwa	tsorba
Desire—thirst ...	trishna	sédpa	srédpa
Prehension	upadana	lénpa	lénpa
Existence (becoming) ...	bhava	sidpa	srid pa
Birth	jati	kyéwa	skyé ba
Old age—Death ...	jara—marana	ga—shi	rga—shi

The terms used in this enumeration lead themselves easily to the vicissitudes of individual lives,
and this is usually the interpretation accepted by the
Hinayanist Buddhists (the Theravadins of the
Southern School). For them, the series of twelve
causes concern individuals: men or animals, but
more especially human beings.

I remember having provoked astonishment and
formal denials from Sinhalese and Burmese Buddhist Monks by hinting that the "Chain of Interdependent originations" could—at least in its principal line—apply to the evolution of a plant as well as
to that of man.

In reality, although the well-read among them
deny it, some of those who call themselves Buddhists—Mahayanists of the Northern countries as
well as Theravadins of the South—have practically
remained attached to the belief in a *jiva*,[4] that is to
say in an *ego*, an entity which transmigrates from
life to life, forsaking its material body at the moment
of death "as one throws away wornout clothing to
put on new clothes".[5]

---

[4] The equivalent of that which Westerners call the soul. *Jīvātman*
is the principle which gives life to the body, and that which, according to the Hindus, is reincarnated. The *Jīvātman* is, according to
the Vedanta, the Paramātman in its individualised form.
[5] Bhagavad Gîta II, 22.

This belief is, however, formally and continually denied by the Doctrine of the Buddha, of which Doctrine the negation of the *ego* is the fundamental article and marks it off from the orthodox Hindu doctrines.

The Buddhist creed, as a matter of fact, consists of two short, incisive statements:

"All aggregates are impermanent"
"All things are devoid of self (atman: "ego" or "soul")".

This means that if we discard the component elements which form that which we call a man, a horse, a tree, a mountain, a star, or no matter what, if we abstract the qualities which make them perceptible to us, we discover nothing which is distinct from these constituent elements, from these qualities, we do not, in any way, find the man, the horse, the mountain *in itself*. These names apply only to a collection of elements.

The classic example given in Buddhist Texts is that of the waggon which consists of a collection of wheels and their spokes, a pole and so forth, . . . or the house which consists of a frame made of beams, of rafters, of a roof and so forth . . . but the *waggon* in itself, the *house* in itself, where are they? . . .

In the same way, if from a man you take away the physical form, sensation, perception, mental activity and consciousness, what remains? Where will you find the man existing in himself outside the corporality and mentality?

In the Secret Teachings great importance is attached to propounding this negation of the *ego* as a fundamental doctrine. Those who lag behind in the belief in an *ego*, it is said, do not understand the meaning of the Teaching, they are in no way Buddhists, they cannot attain to liberation, to salvation, for without understanding (of a transcendent insight) of this absence of any ego, they will not perceive the means by which to go beyond being and non-being.

None of those who profess Buddhism denies this creed and all repeat it in one language or another[6] but in most cases it is "without having understood the meaning of the Teaching".

To the *ego* which is denied by the Buddhist Scriptures, some have substituted a current of elements making their way as a group, as a bundle, very

---

[6] The original formula in Pali is: *Sabbe sankhārā aniccā ; Sabbe sankhārā dukkhā ; Sabbe sankhārā anattā*, which means: All compounded things are impermanent ; All compounded things are suffering ; All things (everything in general) are devoid of an *ego* (of a "self" of their own). The Tibetans split into two the last part of the statement and say: "There is no *ego* in the individual ; there is no *ego* in anything".

much, apparently, like the *quanta* of a Western science.

This current called santāna[7] in a way plays the part of individual life. The Thera Nyānatiloka[8] stated to me one day that Nirvana consisted in the extinction of this current of activity when it ceased to be nourished by Karmic contributions due to the activity of the individual. According to his opinion, that which we consider to be an individual is a particular current, a special *santāna*. Of course the learned Bhikkhu denied the existence of a *jīva* or *ego* existing apart from the santāna. The phenomena which made up the current were discontinuous events following on in a procession without being attached one to another like a parade of ants.

As for me, this current which seems to flow in isolation while preserving its identity among the numerous other currents, seems to depend on an untenable theory. The Tibetan Masters of the Oral Teachings will not admit it either.

---

[7] *Santāna* is a Sanskrit word meaning a continuous flow, a line, a succession. I have discussed the theory of the *santānas* in "Buddhism: its Doctrines and Methods".

[8] Nyānatiloka is the name "in religion" of an erudite German orientalist who has lived for more than forty years in Ceylon as a Buddhist monk. He has published many books, translations of the Pali Scriptures, of the canon of Southern Buddhism and original works.

Those who interpret the Chain of Originations as relating to the life of the individuals explain it in the two following ways or in some similar manner:

I	II
I—Past Life	**I—Past Life**
Ignorance.	Illusion.
Samskāra (mental activity).	Samskāra = Karma.
II—Present Life	**II—Present Life**
Knowledge.	First moment of a new life, conception.
Material existence—mentality.	The five elements which constitiute existence.
Organs of sense and the mind (sixth sense).	In the embryo before the formation of organs of sense.
Impression received by the senses.	Formation of the organs.
Sensation.	The organs and the consciousness begin to co-operate.
Desire.	Distinct sensations.
Grasping attachment.	Awakening of the sexual instinct: beginning of a new karma.
Actions.	Different pursuits in life. Life, that is to say, different kinds of conscious activity.
III—Future Life	**III—Future Life**
Birth.	Rebirth.
Old age.	New life—old age, Death.

On the contrary, in the works of Mahayanist writers we find interpretations of the *Pratitya Samutpāda* which give a cosmic meaning to it, and at once a question occurs: "Why are the twelve links of the chain of Interdependent Originations understood differently in the Sūtras which mention them and in the philosophic works which explain them?"

Vasubandhu,[9] dealing with this question, replies: "Because in the Sūtras, the Chain of Interdependent Originations is set forth in a popular way for the use of the mass of hearers and in a way suitable, for their degree of understanding, that is to say as relating to individual life, while the works which give explanations of it are aimed at its deep meaning."

Thus we see that Vasubandhu distinguishes between a wholly exoteric explanation and one which goes more deeply into the subject.

The Tibetans have their habitual classification of the outer doctrine *chi* and the inner doctrine *nang*. They add to them the *Sangs wai Damnags* which they consider as a body of secret Doctrines. *Secret in the sense that only especially perspicacious minds can attain them.*

The Masters who expound the Oral Teachings of this category do not fail to advise their pupils to make

---

[9] Tibetan name *Ignen* (spelt *dbyig gnien*). He lived in the fifth century.

themselves familiar with the "inner" interpretation (*nang*) of the Chain of Interdependent Originations.

Its entire signification is stated in technical phraseology in the declaration: *"This existing, that arises"* or again: "There is no real production, only interdependence". An explanatory formula is expressed as follows: "There is nothing which is produced by its own self (which is the cause of its own appearing). Nothing appears which is produced by another thing. Nothing came into existence by chance, but that which comes into being exists in dependence on causes."

The Theory of Interdependent Originations is closely bound up with that of the instantaneousness and impermanency of all phenomena, which consist, as has been mentioned above, of discontinuous flashes of energy. The term "interdependent" indicates also that it is not a matter of a direct line.

Care has to be taken *not* to believe that *this* which exists engenders *that* which arises ; it has not the time to do so, so to speak, because the flashes of energy are of too short duration to permit a real act of production. Moreover, nothing is produced by one single cause ; the combination of several causes is always necessary to bring about a result. The seed without the co-operation of earth, dampness, light, etc. will never become a tree.

The fact that the Theory of Interdependent Originations aims at bringing to light is simply that the
temporary existence of certain phenomena is necessary
in order to bring such and such another phenomenon
into existence.

None of the flashes of energy which constitute
the world manifests itself without depending on the
existence of other flashes of energy as ephemeral as
itself, and which take the place of causes for it on
favourable occasions.

In the Mahayanist interpretation of the Chain of
Interdependent Originations this is broadened. Birth,
decrepitude, death, are no longer represented as the
stages of life in the human individual who is born,
develops, grows old and dies, to be reborn and recom-
mence a similar course, going through the alternations
of agreeable or painful sensations. It is a question of
an universal law of impermanence in virtue of which
everything which arises, being the result of a combination of various elements, must necessarily disinte-
grate when causes, other than those which produced
the constitution of the whole, arise.

The last words addressed by the dying Buddha to
His disciples were: "All that which is produced, composed, is perishable."

The law of impermanence governs the suns to the
depth of fathomless space just as it governs the life of

the tiniest insect or the smallest grain of dust. It is not enough to understand that Birth, Decrepitude and Death happen according to such progression as our weak senses are capable of inregistering. The process is continual in all beings, in all things: in the sun or in the grain of dust, each atom which constitutes it individually lives the perpetual drama of birth, old age and death.

The cycle of Interdependent Origins thus takes place in everything, everywhere, in the infinitely small as in the infinitely great. Its development does not take place progressively in time; the twelve causes listed are always present, co-existent and interdependent, their activity is interconnected, and they only exist one with the other.

In fact, the "Interdependent Origins" are in no way a description of incidents occurring to a being which would exist apart from them. Each being *is* the "chain of interdependent origins" as this latter *is* the universe and outside its activity neither being nor universe exists.

The Master who passes on the Oral Teachings to a pupil does not omit to explain clearly to him the theories which I just have summed up briefly and many others which have been elaborated by the subtle Buddhist philosophers of India and China and by Tibetan authors such as Gampopa, Jamyang

Shespa, various leaders of the Sect of the Sakyapas, and so on. The Master encourages his pupil to study the vast philosophic literature available to him in the libraries of the great Monasteries. He does not scorn learning. He is often himself a distinguished scholar, but the usefulness of learning, in his opinion, does not transcend that of a profitable mental gymnastic calculated to render flexible our intellectual faculties, calculated to bring about critical tendencies, suspicion and doubt, this first step towards investigation and knowledge.

The student is then put in touch with the elements of the *Sang wai Damngag* and new interpretations of the Chain of Interdependent Origins are suggested to him.

From the statement of the first terms: Ignorance, Samskāra, appeal is made to the attention of the pupil.

What is it to be ignorant? It is not to know. However ignorance can never be total. One may not know a certain thing, but at the same time, one knows other things. In the final analysis, he who is aware that he "does not know", possesses by that very fact, the knowledge of his existence, whatever may be its nature.

Cannot we then envisage this incomprehensible

ignorance which begins the series of the Twelve
Causes as being erroneous knowledge, false views?

Instead of imagining Ignorance[10] as a kind of
vague, occult power hidden in the depths of space
and eternity, original source of the sorrowful pilgri-
mage of beings through *samsāra,* can we not recognize
that this "not-knowing" is purely *"our own"* in the
sense that it is an integral part of our being?

What is it that produces ignorance, what is it
that keeps it alive? It is our activity made up of
physical acts and mental acts.

Although based on a philosophical conception of
the world which is entirely different from that which
inspired the author of the Bhagavad Gītā, the Oral
Tibetan Teachings agree with the Hindu poem in
saying:

> "Nothing can remain, not even for a single
> moment, without acting. Everything is compelled
> to do so by the very nature of the elements of
> which it is composed (by the natural functions of
> its being)."[11]

What are the agents which urge us to action?—
They are the senses which produce perceptions and

---

[10] Tibetan: *ma rig pa*=nescience.   Sanskrit: *avidyā* which has
the same meaning.

[11] Bhagavad Gītā III, 5.

sensations, and we have seen in the preceding chapter that our senses give us incorrect information. They lead us into error, and if we are deceived by them we are cultivating ignorance. For lack of access to reality not only do we "not know" but we erect on our wrong information various wrong views, and the structure of a fantastic world.

These mental constructions, based on the irrepressible activity of our mind and on ignorance, are the *samskāra* or "compounds"; the *duched* (hdu byed), that is to say, the "collections", the "assemblages", as the Tibetans name them.

These "collections" are kept up by the faith which we have in their reality and by the use we make of them. It is thus that a kind of illusory reality is given to the world which we build up in holding it to be exterior to ourselves, whereas it emanates from us and dwells in us in dependence on the illusion of which we are the victims.

It is in our own mind that the "Chain of Interdependent Originations" evolves, turning back on itself with these three factors: ignorance—desire—act, supporting one another.

Instead of considering the *pratitya samutpāda* as a law which rules us (an exoteric opinion—*chi*) or holding that we are ourselves this chain of origins "flowing like a stream" (esoteric Teaching—*nang*) we can make a further advance with the Secret Teachings only if we understand that if we *are* the chain, we are at the same time its creator.

"I know you O builder of the house,
From now on you shall build no more."[12]

The pupil is left to meditate on this point and the Master goes on to examine another theory, but a long time may elapse in the interval.

---

[12] Dhammapada, 154.

CHAPTER IV

Having rapidly enquired into what is told us of the "Interdependent Originations" we may return to the examination of the theories concerning "memories" which was begun in Chapter II.

In later Buddhism, that is to say between the Vth and the VIth centuries, an important place has been given to the theories concerning the ālaya vijnāna. These theories were not exactly invented at this period for their seeds already existed previously, but their bringing into prominence and their development were the work of the Doctors of the Mahāyāna.

Ālaya is a Sanskrit word which means dwelling, receptacle, store. We meet it in the well-known name of the high mountain chain which separates India from Tibet: Himālaya, that is to say, dwelling or receptacle of the snows. Ālaya vijnāna is then a receptacle of the consciousness.

The *ālaya vijnāna*, receptacle of consciousness, is not mentioned in Tibet in the popular teachings of an elementary kind. We find it in the kind called *nang*, "inner" teachings, and in the *sangs wai damnags*, teachings which are oral and secret.

What is told us about it?

Every action, either physical or mental, every movement occurring either on the plane of gross matter or on the plane of the mind, causes an emission of energy.[1] To use the established expression, it produces a "seed".[2]

This seed, in the same way as all material seeds, tends—given favourable circumstances—to produce a being[3] of the same species as that of the parent who has transmitted the seed. The seed of an oak tends to produce an oak, the seed of an animal, dog or bird, tends to produce a dog or a bird.

Likewise, the innumerable energy-seeds launched into the universe by Desire, Aversion, Love, Hatred, and the actions caused by these feelings, by attachment to individual existence with the material activity which it excites in order to preserve that individual existence to perpetuate it, to increase its power and enlarge its sphere of action, all these seeds tend to reproduce the counterparts of their parents either psychic or material.

In order that the seed should be sown, it is in no way necessary that the feelings we experience should

---

[1] In Tibetan *choug* or *taal* (*rtsal*) in Sanskrit: *shakti.*

[2] In Tibetan *sabon,* in Sanskrit: *bija.*

[3] By "being" one should not understand only an animated being, but in general, something which exists, which *is,* whatever may be the material or subtle nature of this "something".

be materialized in action. The aspirations which we entertain without realizing them, those also which we restrain, our thoughts of whatever kind they may be, unceasingly give out seeds. Furthermore, the hidden activity, always at work in spite of ourselves in the subconscious part of our being, is one of the most powerful sources from which are thrown out these seeds.

It is necessary to go further, say the Secret Teachings, it is necessary to understand, to grasp, to see that there is not a blade of grass, not a grain of sand[4] which is not a "sower" of seed by the activity of its physical life and by that of a psychic life, peculiar to its species, which we must in no way imagine as similar to our own.

There cannot happen the least movement—in this world which *is* movement—without this movement starting other movements, other manifestations of energy tending to repetitions, in dependence on "memories" (vāsanā) or, as the Tibetans call them, on propensities (pag chang). Each of our physical or mental movements is the fruit of causes coming from

---

[4] The atoms (*dul ten*, spel: *rdul phran*) compared to grains of sand or dust of which the Masters of the Secret Teachings say that each of them is a world which comprises myriads of beings and where a drama of life and deaths, similar to that of which we are aware in our world, takes place.

the whole universe and has its repercussions in the whole universe. Thus opens up the working, without beginning, or end, of the activity which is the Universe.

According to one of the theories concerning the energy-seeds thrown out in the Universe, these are stored up in a receptacle (ālaya) where they remain in the state- of latent energies which, in order to manifest themselves, only await the appearance of suitable conditions, just as the seed stored up in a barn will not develop until it is put in contact with damp earth.

Nevertheless, suitable conditions continually appear ; thus while some seeds flow steadily into the receptacle, other seeds equally steadily flow out in the form of habits, of propensities, of "memories" (vāsanā) either of a physical or of a psychic kind which encourages the repetition of material actions or mental activities which have occurred previously.

What are the "conditions" which allow the germination of the seeds? They are themselves the product of seeds, for nothing exists outside the round of actions and their fruit, of the enchainment of causes and the effects, the cause being the effect of the preceding cause and the effects becoming the cause of another effect.

According to the expression of certain Doctors of

the Mahāyāna, the ālaya is "an uninterrupted river with a continuous current".

This comparison of the "river which flows" takes us far from the idea of an abode or receptacle of the seeds, which calls up rather the idea of immobility, of stagnation.

Others have, however, retained in a greater or lesser degree, in different forms and under different names the idea of immobility. A world which is nothing but movement makes them dizzy, they feel themselves out of their depth and, not finding the solid support to which they long to attach themselves, they imagine it, ending by transforming the *ālaya* into the womb (garbha) containing beings, an equivalent of the Brahman of the Vedanta philosophy.

The Oral Secret Teachings assume a very different position in that they are based on the fundamental impermanence of all phenomena and on the fact that these are compounded of various aggregates. The seeds, products of mental activity which may or may not be associated with a material activity, and which include different elements, cannot be considered permanent. Like all formations they consist of successive, fugitive instants. Hence what sort of receptacle or of abode can one imagine which would contain in a waiting state, that is to say, in a state of

repose, that which is elusive, having no appreciable
duration?

In truth, there exists only the perpetual flow,
both continuous (it never stops) and discontinuous (it
consists of distinct moments), of flashes of force;
causes and effects which engender each other in such
a way that the parent-cause can never know its off-
spring-effect for it disappears while the latter emerges,
or rather, it is its disappearance itself which constitutes its effect: the new phenomenon.

Lending some support to the theory of the *ālayā*
receptacle, Vasubandhu[5] stated: The act ends imme-
diately after being born, thus one cannot admit that
it can itself produce the fruit, but it transmits to the
root of consciousness (*mūla vijnāna*) virtualities, energies or seeds which will produce its fruit. These
virtualities are called *vāsanā* (memory).

It is this "root of consciousness" which receives
the impressions comparable to the receptacle out of
which some have almost made a mystic personality.
We shall see how it is regarded in the Oral Teachings.

However, let us consider a declaration of Hiuen
Tsang[6] raffirming the idea of Vasubandhu that the

---

[5] Vasubandhu, an eminent Buddhist philosopher, who lived
between the 5th and 6th century C.E. Some say during the 4th
century.

[6] Hiuen Tsang, (633), a Chinese Buddhist Monk, philosopher and
great traveller.

fruit is not produced by the act, but is engendered by the intervention of the impression made by the act in the "root of consciousness".

"The fruit is not of the character of the act", says Hiuen Tsang, "for it is not directly engendered by the act".

The Secret Teachings in no way contradict this view. The student has already been warned that the effect is never the product of a single cause, but always of several causes of unequal potency. In so far as the seeds are concerned, they are, from their beginning, compounds, including different elements. Moreover, the environment into which they are thrown is, itself, a mixture of dissimilar elements, so that the seed, before producing an effect, will of necessity undergo many contacts with other seeds, and thus, the "impressions" as Vasubandhu named them, being superimposed in different ways, it will be rare that one will take the exact form of another. Thus, as a result of these contacts, of these super-impositions, seeds and impressions will become more or less different from their original nature.

It follows that the *vāsanās*: memories, seeds, tendencies, habits, and so on never recreate the texture of the past—physical or psychic activities—after an absolutely identical pattern. The pattern which will be the future being influenced by the "memories" will show resemblances, more or less marked, to the pattern of the past, but the copy will never be exactly the same.

This excludes the possibility of any definite prophecy. Some people have thought that if one could know all the causes existing at the present moment, one could foresee their effect and thus behold the picture of the future. This idea is rejected in the Oral Teachings.

Based on the law of universal impermanence, while at the same time upholding the determinist doctrine of the concatenation of causes and effects, these caution the student against the idea that the absolute determinism is within his reach ; the sphere of probabilities is alone accessible to him.

Even supposing that they are all known to him at a given moment and that he could calculate, *at that moment,* the effects which are naturally produced by these causes, *at the moment which follows that one,* these causes will have already undergone modifications as a result of their contact with other causes and forces. Not only will they never be identical with what they were before, but, in reality, other causes of a different kind will have followed them. It follows from this that the effects which may be expected from these last will differ from those which one might have foreseen in the preceding moment.

ALEXANDRA DAVID NEEL
Wearing her monastic robes in Tibet

ALEXANDRA DAVID NEEL
Wearing her monastic robes in Tibet

At the same time, a similar activity takes place in the senses and in the "mind" of the observer which, they too, are renewed from moment to moment.[7]

Which moment, among this double current of fugitive phenomena, could have shown a stable picture of causes suitable to serve as a basis for the exact determination of the elements which make up the face of the future? . . .

*
* *

The Tibetans translate ālaya vijnāna by *kun ji namparshespa*. Is this translation exact?—The discussion of such a question is outside the plan of the present book, but what interests us is the meaning which the Tibetans give to this term in their Secret Teachings.

The idea of a "receptacle" cannot be applied to *Kun ji*. *Ji* (spelt gzi) means base, foundation. Family property is called *ji*. The *ji* of an individual is the dwelling-place which, before becoming his, has been that of the family to which he belongs. In the figurative sense, *ji* can be the basis on which a doctrine is founded. *Ji* is applied also to the foundation of a building, to no matter what on which something is based.

---

[7] See Chapter II.

Kun means simply "all".

As to *namparshespa*, it consists of two words: *nampar* which means "perfectly", and *shespa* which means "to know"—"to be acquainted with".

In short, *kunji namparshespa*, means "acquaintance-knowledge basis of everything".

At this point some explanation is necessary:

First of all we should understand that the knowledge, the consciousness in question, is not at all the superior knowledge called Shesrab.[8]

The knowledge which is put before us as being the basis of everything is that which distinguishes, which separates, allots names, forms, qualities: in short it is that which carries out the arrangements of the world. The world is its work.

That knowledge is a deception; it depends on our senses, each of them providing its contribution to the common fund.

Thus one distinguishes:

Knowledge acquired by the eye . . . form and colour.

Knowledge acquired by the ear . . . sounds.

---

[8] *Shes* = knowledge ; *rab* = superior. A similar difference exists between the Sanskrit words *vijñāna and prajñā*, the first being a discriminatory knowledge applied to things of the world, while the second is transcendent wisdom.

Knowledge acquired by the tongue . . tastes.
Knowledge by the nose . . . odours.
Knowledge acquired by the whole epidermis,
that results from the sensations produced by
touch in contacts.

And as the sixth, and by no means the least
important, the knowledge acquired by the mind,
that is to say by mental contacts: ideas which
one has heard expressed, and so on.

Two other kinds of knowledge are also mentioned; their meaning is widely different from
Sanskrit words listed in the list of the *vijñānas* drawn
up by the savants of Indian Buddhism. One of them
is shown as the sum of the six forms of knowledge
listed above, it is the knowledge or understanding
which is possessed by the darkened mind (*niön
mongpa tchen gy yid kyi namparshespa*).[9] In fact, it
is false knowledge: it is the error which dominates
that mind which is incorrectly informed by the senses
which pass on to it their impressions. These impressions are always falsified by their inability to grasp
reality.

The understanding knowledge of the "darkened
mind" is the ally of the "understanding knowledge

---

[9] Spelling: *nyong mongs pas tchan gyi kyi rnam par shespa.*
translating the Sanskrit ādana vijnāna.

which grasps" (*len pai namparshespa*). The false notions which are held by the darkened shadowed mind are grasped, assembled and become motives inciting the action. A mental activity based on wrong knowledge builds up, on its data, an image of the world which has no relation to reality.

It is this world which we watch like a play which unfolds outside of ourselves while, in fact, there is nothing there but a canvas bearing many coloured patterns, which we have woven and printed in ourselves according to the indications of our erroneous knowledge.

Thus, the *Kun ji namparshespa* made up of the contributions of all the *namparshespa* is in no way a mythical receptacle, but our own consciousness, the basis of the phenomenal world, the whole of *our* universe.

The "river" with the current both continuous and discontinuous made up of "seeds" is nothing else than our mind in which the *namparshespa*, understanding-knowledge, ideas, and so on which they arouse appear and disappear in series of separate moments, but arising constantly.

At this point the Master who is passing on to a pupil the Secret Teachings, puts a question to him: What do you mean by "your mind" when you speak of it, when you think of it?

To express that which we call "mind" the Tibetans have available three words which are not fully interchangeable. They are: *sems, Yid* and *lo* (*blo*).

Lo includes all the moods of the mind, agitated or calm, attentive, searching, listless, indifferent, impressionable or insensitive to exterior impressions, inclined towards discrimination, towards classification or unaware of differences, the imaginative mind, or the mind solely occupied by the facts within reach, the understanding or the dull mind, the agitated passionate or unimpressionable mind, the mind which works over ideas, collects them, reasons, the humbled, depressed or alert mind, etc., all the forms in which the mind shows itself.

Yid means more especially the mind considered as pure intellect.

Sems has usually a wide application as the "thinking principle" which distinguishes animated beings from things considered to be inert. *Sems,* as it is understood exoterically, has a meaning which comes close to *Namshes* i.e., the "consciousness" which transmigrates (the *jiva* of the Indians). *Sems tchen* (having sense or mind) is an expression which, in the literary language, means all animated beings, including man, but in popular speech only animals are thus called and to employ it of a man would be insulting.

The student of the Secret Teachings is, in most cases, taught the various meanings of the three words indicating the three aspects of the mind, so he understands the questions put to him when the Master, using the generic term *sems* asks him: What do you mean by "your mind" when you speak of it, when you think of it?

In order to enable the pupil to perceive the diversity and the momentary nature of that which we call "mind" the Master insists on the different moods of it, some of which have been listed above. Just as the idea of an *"ego"* existing apart from the elements which constitute it, has been disproved, so that of a mind existing apart from these moods, these forms of activity which manifest it, is equally denied.

Is it not this "mind" to which moods and forms of activity are attributed, while not identifying it with them, that most men take for their real and lasting *"ego"*?—

Yet according to the statements which the Buddhist Scriptures attribute to the Buddha:

"It would be better to consider the body as an "ego" than to consider the mind as such, for the body seems to last for a year, two years or a hundred years, but that which is called mind,

thought or knowledge, appears and disappears in
a perpetual state of change.

Just as a monkey gambolling in the forest
grasps a branch, then lets it go to seize another,
so that which is called mind, thought or knowledge, appears and disappears in a perpetual
change, day and night."[10]

The student studying the Secret Teachings has
not only already familiarized himself with these
theories, but he has tested their exactitude.

During his meditations, while watching his mind
with close attention, he has attained *Lhag Thong*
and "seeing more" than most men, he has contem-
plated the continual arising and disappearance of
ideas, of volitions, of memories, and so on, which pass
like a procession of short-lived bubbles floating down
a river. He has realised for himself that "mind" is
only a word indicating a series of mental phenomena.

Despite everything, the deeply-rooted habit of
thinking on the basis of an *"ego"* may tend to cause
him to narrow the extent of the mind. Thus, while
holding it to be a current of transitory moments he
may, at the same time, accept either consciously or
unconsciously, the theory of the *santānas*, isolated

---

[10] Samyutta Nikāya.

currents of consciousness and of mental operations, following individually their courses.

Now according to the Secret Teachings, what must be understood, seen, felt, is that there does not exist any current which is *my* mind, and therefore it follows that there is not a plurality of currents which are the minds of other individuals, but only a single current which is *Kunji namparshespa,* the sum of all mental activity at work without any cognizable beginning. It is in this totality that what we call *our* mind is immersed, our mind which we try so hard to separate and define. Furthermore, this effort is useless. Whether we are aware of it or not, the thoughts, the desires, the needs which we feel for life, our thirst for it—nothing of all this is completely ours, for all of it is collective, it is the flowing river of incalculable moments of consciousness having its source in the impenetrable depths of eternity.

Here is found again, in another form, the conception of the *Alaya vijñāna,* a mixture of "seeds". themselves the fruit of acts, determining new acts by the effect of "memories" as the Indians say, or, as expressed by the Tibetans, of "tendencies".

Nevertheless it is not enough to listen to the teaching of such things or to read an explanation of them in philosophic works. They must be seen, *seen* by oneself as a result of perspicacious insight, the penetrating vision *lhag thong* which causes one to see more than we have seen up to the present.

Lhag thong, the transcendent insight which sees beyond appearances and penetrates below the surface is able, like any other faculty, to be developed and cultivated. It is for us to do this, and so to prepare ourselves for the most fascinating of explorations.

CHAPTER V

The most striking of the Tibetan Buddhist doctrines that which is specially noteworthy in the Secret Teachings concern the *"going beyond"*. This doctrine is based on the Prajñā Pāramitā to which the great work of Nāgārjuna is consecrated.

The Tibetans, like the Chinese, have given to the term Prajñā Pāramitā a very different meaning from that which is attributed to it by the Indian authors, and which was adopted from them by most Western Orientalists.

According to the latter, Prajñā Pāramitā means excellent wisdom, the best, the highest wisdom whereas, for the Chinese, it is question of a wisdom which is "gone beyond", according to the Prajñā Pāramitā mantram which is recited in all countries professing Mahāyāna Buddhism:

"O Wisdom which has gone beyond, gone beyond the beyond, to Thee homage".[1]

However, while this mantram shows us a wisdom "which has gone beyond"—gone to "the other shore" as Chinese say—Tibetans translate Prajñā Pāramitā

---

[1] gate, gaté, paramgaté, parasamgaté Bodhi, Swahā! (Pronounced as with a French *é* and not as *gate* (a door) in English.

by: *"sherab kyi pharol tu chinpa"*[2] that is to say: "going beyond wisdom".

The genitive particle *kyi* leaves no doubt as to the meaning intended by the translator. To express that Wisdom accomplishes the act of going, he ought to have written *kyis*. But, more than any grammatical consideration, the fact that a whole doctrine is based on the precept of "going beyond" shows us the spirit in which the Tibetans understand the Prajñā Pāramitā.

It has seemed to me necessary to give my readers these explanations, because those among them who are familiar with Buddhist literature may be surprised at the manner in which the "excellent virtues" which they have met in the course of their reading are considered here.

The number of these was originally six; later, four other "virtues" were added to the list, but these latter only play a secondary part.[3]

In this list, each "virtue" is treated in the same way as the wisdom-knowledge (*shesrab*), that is to say that its name is followed by the words "to go beyond". So, while in the works of those authors who take the translation of *pāramitā* as "excellent" we find: excellent charity, excellent morality, etc. . . . the

---

[2] Tibetan spelling: *pharol tu phyinpa.*

[3] See following table.

Tibetans tell us: "to go beyond charity, to go beyond wisdom-knowledge".

The "Excellent Virtues" or, for the Tibetans, those beyond which one must go are:

	Sanskrit	Tibetan
Gift	Dāna	djinpa (sbynpa)
Morality	Sīla	tsul tim (tsul grims)
Patience	Khānti	seupa (bsod pa)
Energy, effort	Vīrya	tsundus (brtson hgrus)
Meditation, concentration of mind	Dhyāna	samten (bsam gtan)
Transcendent Wisdom ...	Prajñā	shesrab (shes rab)

With the addition of the four "Virtues" added later:

Method, skilfulness of means	Upāya	thabs
Aspirations, good wishes[4] ...	Pranidhāna	meunlam (smonlam)
Strength, vigour	Balādhāna	tob (stobs)
Knowledge, learning ...	Jnāna	yeshes

Is it a good thing to possess these virtues and to practise them? Obviously yes, but none of them taken by itself nor all of them together are able to produce liberation (*tharpa*). The righteous man, the saint, as much as the wicked man and the criminal remain prisoners in the round (samsāra)[5] of birth and

---

[4] Very wrongly translated as "prayer" by certain Western authors. In the same sense that it is understood in the West, "prayer" has no place in Buddhism.

[5] The Sanskrit word *samsāra* is, in Tibetan, *korwa* (*skorwa*); its meaning, the "round", being identical.

death, of assemblages and dissolutions, which makes
up the illusory world of phenomena although, in the
round, the fate of the first-named may differ from
that of the second.

According to the popular religious beliefs, the
practice of these virtues leads to happy rebirths in
the world of men or in the worlds of the Gods, while
evil acts lead to unhappy rebirths in those spheres
where suffering is reigning. The masses of Tibetans
hardly look beyond these two kinds of future, nevertheless the idea that salvation, deliverance from
samsāra, the state of illumination of a Buddha are
very different things from the practice of virtue and
the carrying out of religious rites, is not wholly
foreign to them. That is a question, the good people
of the Land of the Snows think, quite beyond their
intelligence, and they do not stop to examine it.

At a higher degree, that of the teaching called
nang (esoteric), it is explained that to be "excellent"
the virtues and their practice must have become
integrated in our character. They must be unconscious, have developed into reflex actions. Thus the
act of helping a suffering being ought to occur as
spontaneously, as instinctively as the act of pulling
back one hand quickly if it touches anything red-hot.

If our charity, our patience, our effort, etc. in
fact, no matter which of the excellent virtues, only

manifest itself after a mental process has shown us
the usefulness of it, or the necessity of forcing ourselves to it through obedience to certain moral principles which we have been taught to respect, then the
actions which we accomplish may be beneficial for
those who are their object. We, however, shall only
benefit from them as an educational exercise which
is likely to turn us into robots, moved by agencies
exterior to ourselves. The deeper part of our being
would not have been modified, and such transforma-
tion is the only thing that counts.

Buddhist salvation, Liberation, consists in a
fundamental change in our perceptions, in our ideas,
in our feelings ; it is an awakening resulting from
transcendent and profound insight (*lhags thong*)
which causes us to "see more" and to discover, beyond
the world of virtues and vices, of Good and Evil, a
sphere where these pairs of opposites do not exist. It
is a question, after having practised the "excellent
virtues", of going beyond them because the transcendent insight has shown them to be puerile, senseless,
unfounded and ineffective.

The doctrine of "Going Beyond" in conjunction
with those of the "Direct Path" and of "Sudden
Liberation" form the veritable core of the teachings
of the Higher Degree which are called secret teachings, and those who have been initiated into them or

who have understood their exactitude are advised
not to spread them lightly as they are dangerous for
the mass of men whose intelligence is too limited to
grasp their real meanings.

Ought we to consider the collection of doctrines
and theories which together make up the secret
teaching as being essentially and uniquely Tibetan?
—That would be somewhat risky. Ideas hardly ever
spring up from a single centre. In particular periods
we see similar ideas arise among men separated by
great distances and without there having been any
material contact between them. However, as far as
Tibet is concerned, we cannot neglect the possibility
of direct or indirect relations between the Tibetan
thinkers and living philosophers (or those who had
lived) on their frontiers: Chinese or Indian.

The famous Buddhist philosopher Nāgārjuna
has eloquently proclaimed the Middle Way (Madhyamika) which leans neither towards affirmation nor
towards negation because these only exist relatively
to each other, and so, in consequence, neither one
nor the other has any independent reality of its own.
One has to go beyond the idea of "yes" and "no", of
"being" as that of "non-being", says Nāgārjuna.
"Wisdom" must "go beyond" all conceptions, or, as
it is translated by the Tibetans, we must go beyond

Wisdom (*i.e.*, Wisdom as we conceive it) which comes, in the end, to the same thing.

Long before Nāgārjuna the Buddha had already laid down the principles of a similar spiritual and intellectual discipline. Speaking to one of his disciples, he said to this effect:

> "Men are accustomed to state *"is"* or *"is not"* but for him who perceives wisely and according to the truth how all things are brought about in the world, for such an one there is no *"is not"*. And for him who perceives wisely and in truth how the things in the world perish, for him there is no "is".[6]

> "*Everything is,* is one of the extremes, *nothing is,* is the other. I teach, between the two, the truth of the Interdependent Originations."[7]

That is to say that everything which exists depends, for its existence, on the existence of other things which produce it or which support it, and that the existence of that which exists ceases when the causes or the conditions which support it themselves cease. Thus, all existence is relative. One cannot

---

[6] Or more exactly, in Tibetan, there is no "existence" (yöd) there is no "non existence" (med)—Asti and nāsti in Sanskrit—both are denied.

[7] Samyutta Nikāya.

say that it *is*, because it is not autogenous, nor, on the other hand, can one consider it as pure nothingness.

"To go beyond" is, in fact, to cease to cling to the opinions, the connections which belong to the world of illusion, and to understand that they have only a relative value depending on things which themselves have only a relative existence but which we should be wrong to consider as absolutely non-existent.

The Masters who, in Tibet, claim to be the possessors of the Secret Teachings[8] and who are recognised as such, never pretend that the doctrines they set forth to small groups of selected disciples, have been wholly worked out in Tibet itself. On the contrary, they state that these doctrines and the disciplines attached thereto date back to the distant past, well before the oldest period mentioned in Tibetan history. If they sometimes attribute the origin of the transmission of the Secret Teachings to mythical personages such as Dordji Tchang, they admit without difficulty that this is a picturesque way of expressing the fact that the beginnings of these teachings are unattainable by our researches, and that the spirit of these teachings has always, either in one world or in another, inspired an élite of thinkers who were

---

[8] *Sang wai damnag (gsang bai gdam snag).*

particularly perspicacious, and who "saw beyond" (*lhags thong*) that which appeared to the majority of beings.

As far as we are concerned, leaving aside all groundless assumptions we must recognize that the inner history of the religious and philosophic evolution of the Tibetans is not well known to us, in fact we may say that it is unknown. The documents which we possess are of relatively recent date, and hardly tell us anything beside the founding and propagation of Buddhism in the country by missionaries belonging to different Mahāyānist or Tantric schools. Yet other influences may have been at work in Tibet, either before the coming of Buddhism, or at the period during which took place the building-up of this composite body of philosophic and mystical theories and of popular religion which people of the West call Lamaism.

The Böns[9] overcome by the Lamaist clergy and who now copy the latter in many ways as far as the white Böns are concerned, or who are only, with rare exceptions, simple sorcerers as far as the black Böns are in question, have probably included in the past some enlightened adepts of Taoist teachings. We still occasionally meet in Tibet some examples of

---

[9] Pronounced *Peune*. More correctly, the Bön pos, followers of the Bön religion who are likened by the Chinese to the Taoists.

these thinkers among the anchorites, although these would not claim to be Taoists.

Examining the theories belonging to the Secret Teachings the question arises whether certain among them, such as that of non-action coupled in these teachings with the doctrines of "going beyond", of the direct path and of sudden illumination, have not entered as a result of contact with Chinese Taoists. This is evidently only a guess and we ought not to concentrate our attention only on these latter.

Tibetan Masters of mysticism often mention teachings of nothern origin which have been mysteriously transmitted. These enigmatic sayings seem to be based rather on legend than on historical fact. Moreover we ought not to take the word "northern" in the geographical sense. In Tibet, as in India, "north" has mystical meaning.

On the other hand, some Indians including the learned Mr. Tilak believe in the nordic origin of the Āryas[10] whose cradle was, according to them, situated in the arctic regions. This would explain, by the persistent effect of atavistic memories, the

---

[10] It should be remembered *ārya* means honourable, venerable, noble. The ancestors of the white race now called the Aryan Race called themselves "nobles" in scorn to the people of other races, just as the Germans called themselves Noble race (Heren volk).

fascination which is exercised by the north on some of their mystics.

This explanation cannot apply to Tibet where this same fascination is also found and even to a higher degree. In the Tibetan legends numerous allusions are made to a northern country where the transcendental doctrines originated. Certain *nald-jorpas*[11] pretend to go there occasionally. Enlightened Tibetans believe that this is a matter of phychic experiences, occurring in the course of special meditations, and not of actual voyages.

On the historical or semi-historical level, the Tantric doctrines are, in the opinion of certain learned men, considered to have been imported into Bengal by travelling merchants coming from the North. In such a case what North can be in question?—From Tibet or from Kashmir, lying to the north of India, or from regions farther away and stretching beyond Tibet?—We lack valid and precise information on this point. Moreover, it belongs to the domain of historical research and, as such, is outside the scope of the present book, so I cannot discuss it at greater length.

Let us return then to the doctrines propounded

---

[11] Literally "he who possesses peace, serenity". This is the name of Tibetan Yogins.

to students admitted to initiation in the Secret Teachings.

Is the doctrine of "going beyond", which has been roughly sketched above, definitive? The Masters of the Secret Teachings say that it leads a long way, but if you ask them categorically: "Does it lead to the Goal?" they will only smile and remain silent.

The word Goal, as also the idea of a Goal, *i.e.*, a final, absolute objective, is not used in the Secret Teachings. Both are abandoned in going beyond the limit of the "Inner" teachings (*nang*).

The Masters of the Secret Teachings will willingly remind their pupils of the ancient Buddhist parable of the raft.

The traveller who finds his road blocked by a river will use a raft to reach the opposite shore, but, this shore once reached, he will not carry the raft on his shoulders while continuing his journey. He will abandon it as something which has become useless.

This raft represents the different kinds of methods, intellectual training or moral discipline, which are available as means to bring the seeker of liberation to the "other shore". On this shore, both have lost their value ; they bear no relation to the conditions existing on the "other shore" and, like the raft in the parable, they are only a useless burden.

In any case, this "other shore" is itself only a figurative expression, it is nowhere and it is everywhere.

The "other shore" is that which is "beyond" all our conceptions and this is why it is equivalent to *shesrab pharol to chinpa,* the going beyond everything of the highest kind: transcendent wisdom because it also is a conception of our mind and nothing more than a raft facilitating the crossing; the best, the surest of rafts, but which the transcendent insight (*lhag thong*) shows as what it is in reality, that is to say, an instrument.

Moreover, does the reaching of the other bank mean the attainment of a definite goal?—This is what the majority of Buddhists believe. However the point of view in the Secret Teachings is different.

The man who has crossed the river will, perhaps, rest a while on the shore which he has reached, but beyond that point extends a country to be traversed, so the man will arise and continue that journey. The crossing of the river, the landing on the "opposite bank" are but a stage.

Stage towards what destination? Taoist mystics have left us an enigmatic declaration to which the Masters of the Secret Teaching fully subscribe when, in a slightly different form, they pose the problem to their pupils.

"The country which is nowhere is the real home."[12]

On the other hand, is there any traveller who makes a crossing? Is there a *somebody* who reaches the other shore?

If this was the case, this traveller would carry with him the "hither shore" into the "beyond", just as the dust on the soles of one's shoes is carried from one place to another. The traveller would transform the "other bank" into "this bank" because *here* and *there* are in him, *are him* and that outside the mind which thinks "here" and "there" are no other "here" and "there".

To go beyond virtue and vice, opinions and beliefs[13] is to go beyond the mental constructions which are built up by the mind, unceasingly, and to recognize, by transcendent insight, that they are void of reality. It is also to recognize, by transcendent insight, that *that which* has been imagined as practising virtue, surrendering to vice, as holding opinions and elaborating theories, as travelling towards a goal and reaching the goal, is nothing but an inconsistent phantom, devoid of reality.

---

[12] This sentence is ascribed to the Chinese Master Lü tzü.

[13] To one of his disciples who asked him: "If I am questioned about the opinions held by my Master, what should I say?", the Buddha replied: "You shall say: the Venerable One holds no opinions, he is free from all opinions."

CHAPTER VI

The Secret Oral Teachings associate with the doctrine of "going beyond" those of non-activity, of the direct path, and of sudden illumination. More exactly, they consider these last as being included in the "going beyond" as particular aspects of it.

Passing "beyond" is equivalent to liberation and the three above-mentioned theories directly concern it.

But first of all what is liberation as it is viewed in the Secret Teachings?

We know that Buddhist salvation consists in deliverance from the round of successive deaths and births in a perpetual voyage comprising numerous painful incidents, in the course of which we are united to that which we detest and separated from that which we love. At least such is an exoteric description of salvation, current among Buddhists.

This deliverance has been named *Nirvāna*, a word well-known to all those who are in the least familiar with Buddhist literature.

The literal meaning of *Nirvāna* is extinction and because of this signification the most erroneous ideas have been spread concerning the nature of Buddhist salvation. This is not the place to examine these false interpretations.   Two words will suffice.   The answer to those that imagine that Buddhist salvation consists in the annihilation of the "ego", at the death of the "person", is that, as Buddhism denies the existence of an *"ego"* or a soul, whatever be the name given to it, there cannot be any question of the annihilation of *that* which is held to be non-existent.

In reality there is annihilation but it is that of false views, of ignorance, and more exactly of the belief in the existence of an *"ego"* which is independent, homogeneous and permanent, a belief which deforms our understanding of the world in deforming our mental vision.

The Tibetans have not translated the word *Nirvāna*. Not because they were not capable of doing so, but probably because the idea of salvation appeared to them somewhat differently from that which obtained in other Buddhist schools of philosophy.

Their equivalent for *Nirvāna* is the phrase *"gone beyond suffering"*[1] This has not the solemnity of the word *Nirvāna*; it is currently used to say that a high religious dignitary is dead, without necessarily implying that the dead man had attained perfect spiritual illumination and had become a Buddha.

To express this last idea, not only as regards a

---

[1] *Nia nieun les despa*, spelt *mya nyen las hdas pa*.

dead man but often too of a living individual, the
Tibetans say simply "to have become Buddha", "he
has become a Buddha", or "he is a Buddha".[2]

However, the term most commonly used alike in
the spoken language as in literature is: *liberation*
(*tharpa*) or the expression: *"to be liberated"* (*thar
song*).

There is no idea of death in this idea of liberation. One frees oneself in one's present life and
without leaving it.[3]

On the other hand the Buddhists of the Southern
Schools of the Theravadins are inclined to believe
that the enlightened man dies, if not instantaneously
at least after a short delay after having become an
Arhan, i.e., after having attained spiritual illumination.

In the same way the Theravadins (Hinayanists)
differentiate between the state to which an *Arhan* has
attained when enlightened and the state of Buddha-
hood, and also between *Nirvāna* reached in this life,
as was the case of the Buddha, and a *parinirvāna*
attained after death.

These distinctions are known to the Masters of

---

[2] *Sangs-gyaipa* (sangs rgyas pa) often shortened to *sangs gya* in
current language.

[3] The Secret Teachings insist on the instantaneous character of
liberation and the possibility of attaining it in the present life as
accomplished by the Buddha.

the Secret Teachings, but they brush them aside,
considering them among the "mental compositions"
whose author is our mind, and "beyond" which one
must go.

*

*   *

The Masters of the Secret Teachings state that
the theories concerning non-activity (tös méd)[4] have
been transmitted from master to disciple, in their
lines, from time immemorial.

In support of their assertions we should note that
a doctrine of non-action known by the name of *wu-
wei* has been equally honoured in China from very
ancient times. However the manner in which is
understood the non-action is not the same in the
Tibetan Teachings as that which was current among
the ancient Taoists or the Chinese mystics who
preceded them.

Liberation is achieved by the practice of non-
activity, say the Masters of the Secret Teachings.

What is, according to them, non-activity?—Let
us first of all notice that it has nothing in common
with the quietism of certain Christian or oriental
mystics. Ought one to believe that it consists in
inertia and that the disciples of the Masters who

---

[4] Tibetan spelling: *spros méd*.

honour it are exhorted to abstain from doing anything whatever?—Certainly not.

In the first place, it is impossible for a living
being to do nothing. To exist is, in itself, a kind of
activity. The doctrine of non-action does not in any
way aim at those actions which are habitual in life:
eating, sleeping, walking, speaking, reading, studying,
etc. In contradistinction to the Taoist mystics who,
in general, consider that the practice of non-activity
requires complete isolation in a hermitage, the
Masters of the Secret Teachings, although prone to
appreciate "the joys of solitude", do not consider
them in any way indispensable. As for the practice
of non-activity itself, they judge it absolutely necessary
for the production of the state of deliverance (*tharpa*).

In the preceding chapter it was said that neither
the practice of any particular virtue nor that of
numerous virtues together can bring liberation. This
fact is constantly recalled to the pupils by the Masters
who explain the traditional Secret Oral Teaching to
them. They never tire of repeating the classic simile
of the two chains. Whether one is bound by an iron
chain or by a golden chain means, in both cases, to
be bound. The activity used in the practice of virtue
is the chain of gold while that utilized in evil deeds
is the iron chain. Both imprison the doer.

The Dhammapada which forms part of the

canonical literature of the Southern School of Buddhism, and which can be considered as representing
the original Buddhist doctrine, also stresses the two
chains and the necessity of breaking them.

"He who has shaken off the two chains, that
of good and that of evil, he is a Brāhman."[5]

The word Brāhmana is taken, in this text, in the
old Indian meaning of "he who has acquired the
knowledge of the Brāhman", that is to say of the
Absolute Being, the Supreme Truth. This is the
spiritually enlightened man who has "gone beyond"
the phantasmagoria of *samsāra*.

What then is this activity from which one ought
to abstain?—It is the disordered activity of the mind
which, unceasingly, devotes itself to the work of a
builder erecting ideas, creating an imaginary world
in which it shuts itself like a chrysalis in its cocoon.

It is this same work of a builder which was
meant by the author of the Yoga Sūtras when he
wrote: "Yoga is the suppression of the movements
of the mind".[6]

In the same way Tsong Khapa[7], the founder of

---

[5] Dhammapada, 412.

[6] Yoga citta vritti nirodha.

[7] Tsong Khapa was born about 1356 in Amdo, a Tibetan district
now included in the Chinese frontier district of Chinghai. A large

the Sect of the Gelugs pas (commonly known as the
"Yellow Caps") who probably was initiated in the
Secret Teachings, postulated the same necessity for
the suppression of this "restlessness of the thoughts
and the seeds to which it is due".

A similar opinion was expressed by Chandra-
kīrti.[8] According to him "the essence of Nirvāna
consists simply in the extinction of the constructive
activity of our imagination".

No external agent forges the chains, either of
gold or of iron, no one employs them to bind us to
the world of illusion. It is the ideas which we hold
and not our material activity, in itself, which con-
structs the chains and binds us with them.

Why is this mental activity, calculated on false
data, an obstacle to liberation?—Simply because it is
this activity, builder of mental constructions,[9] of
castles in the air, which, incessantly, builds afresh

---

monastery has been built in the place of his birth. The author of
the present book lived several years there with her adopted son the
Lama Yongden.

[8] Chandrakirti (about the end of the sixth century or the beginning of the seventh.) Sometimes thought to be the eighth century,
but this appears to be an error. His Tibetan name is Dawa Tagspa
(Zlawa grags pa). When he went to Tibet he was a professor in the
monastic university of Vikramasila in the country of Magadha, India.

[9] At this point the statement which constitutes the first article
of the Chain of Interdependent Originations should be noted "On
ignorance depend the mental constructions (samskaras)".

the edifice of the world of illusion in which we are prisoners, and that, outside of our mind which creates it, this world does not exist.

The Master of the Secret Teachings concludes here: That which is necessary is to enter into the "Way of seeing" (*thong lag*). This way is that in which the facts are examined and analysed with constant attention, and where no room is left for the wandering of the imagination.

On this way, *lhag thong*, the transcendent insight is constantly employed, and it continually perfects itself with exercise.

Such is the conception of non-activity in the Secret Teachings. There is thus no question of developing material or spiritual inertia to which one would force oneself, this coercion would require an effort, and so would be a form of activity. It suffices to allow the current of existence to flow freely without attempting to prevent or guide it, watching it like an interested spectator, may be amused, but always detached although feeling one with the spectacle, immersed in the current and flowing with it.

"Path of Seeing" (Thong Lam) is another name for the "Direct Path". The Tibetans describe this picturesquely, as a steep path climbing the precipitous side of a mountain so as to reach the summit quickly, while a wide and well-built road rises by

easy gradients circling the mountain. The first is a
break-neck path fit for mountaineers who are sure-
footed; the other suits leisurely strollers who, in
truth, do not dream of dizzy heights and hardly aim
at such exploits.

The long road is still that on which the pilgrims
linger to polish up the golden chain of virtues. The
majority of these imagine that in this way they
progress, without difficulties and without risks, towards
a future which they generally fancy as a happy re-
birth in this world, in pleasant conditions or in a
heavenly realm.[10]

Even those who have formed a more correct
view, although a vague one, of what may be liberation, Nirvāna, do not easily give up the belief that
one can, gradually and safely, move towards it by
the long road of holiness. They may be heard to
admit the excellence of the direct road, but they say
that it is dangerous because the guard-rails of social,
moral and religious laws are missing from its edge,
and the traveller who makes a false step risks a fall
into an abyss.

It may, indeed, be foolish to preach to an individual of ordinary mind that there is neither Good
nor Evil, that his acts have no importance, and that.

---

[10] Compare Chapter V, page 77.

moreover, he is not the author of them because he is moved by causes whose miscellaneous origins are lost in the inscrutable night of eternity.

The man with a common mind—with an "infantile" mind as the Tibetans politely say—cannot understand the co-existence of the two worlds: that of the Absolute and the Void and that of relativity in which he, the pilgrim, makes his life's journey.

In contradiction with current opinion, the Masters of the Secret Teachings do not hesitate to declare to those of their disciples who are judged capable of understanding this revelation: "The Gradual Way, the persevering cultivation of the virtues, of holiness, do not lead to liberation". The greatest saint, even if he has sacrificed a thousand times all that he held most dear, even his life itself, for love of others, for that of a God or for a noble ideal, remains a prisoner of *samsāra* if he has not understood that all that is a childish game, empty of reality, a useless phantasmagoria of shadows which his own mind projects on the infinite screen of the Void.

On the direct road, this understanding is attained without any apparent preparation. The climber has not hesitated to lean over the abyss on which the path borders, he has not hesitated sometimes to descend into them so as to inspect the depths, he has known how to climb up out of them, and then, suddenly, one day as a result of something apparently without any importance: the colour of a flower, the form of the branch of a tree, a cloud, a bird's song, the yapping of a jackal, the howling of a distant wolf or even a simple pebble against which he struck his foot in passing, and there arises a vision in his mind, *lhag thong,* transcendent insight is born.

No grandiloquent description of the nature of this insight is to be expected. No scene of fairyland is promised for the contemplation of the disciple following the Direct Path, the Secret Teachings are expressed in sober language suited to the subjects in question. Illumination is the discovery of the reality existing beneath appearances, and he who is enlightened will be aware of the place which he, in fact, occupies in this reality.

That suffices ; he will cease to be the dupe of a mirage ; ceasing to create it, he will have broken the chains and will be liberated—*thar song.*

Like other religions, the Buddhism of the Southern School (Hīnayāna) tends to offer to its adepts a dark picture of the world. If the Christians consider this world a "vale of tears", the faithful of the Hīnayāna are told to meditate on the repulsive aspect of the body considered as a bag containing a stomach, intestines, etc. . . . filled with foul substances: bile, urine, excrements, etc. . . . . the result sought being that of producing disgust and so combat all attachment to the physical form and to sensuality.

The position of the Secret Teachings is wholly different. There is no attempt to provoke disgust on the part of the pupil. Dislike is only a form of attachment upside down, and both have the same effect: that of blinding the person who feels them to that to which he has given importance in allowing it to occupy his mind.

No special feeling towards anything is laid down in the Secret Teachings. The Master expects the pupil who has examined the questions to which his attention has been drawn, to find there reasons for a serene indifference. If he cannot refuse to play a role in the comedy or drama of the world, at least he understands that it is all a game. If it has fallen to him to personify a king, a great man, a famous scientist, he will not be proud of himself; if he must play the part of a poor wretch, an ignorant man, he is not ashamed of himself. He knows that these differences only exist on the stage and that, once the play is over, the actors will be stripped of the used costumes in which they have been seen.

The Secret Teachings lead the pupil farther. They teach him to look, with the same serene indifference, at the incessant working of his mind and

the physical activity displayed by the body. He
ought to succeed in understanding, in noting that
nothing of all that is *from him*, is *him*. *He*, physi-
cally and mentally, is the multitude of others.

This "multitude of others" includes the material
elements—the ground, one might say—which he owes
to his heredity, to his atavism, then those which he
has ingested, which he has inhaled from before his
birth, by the help of which his body was formed, and
which, assimilated by him, have become with the
complex forces inherent in them, constituent parts of
his being.

On the mental plane, this "multitude of others"
includes many beings who are his contemporaries:
people he consorts with, with whom he chats, whose
actions he watches. Thus a continual inhibition is
at work while the individual absorbs a part of the
various energies given off by those with whom he is
in contact, and these incongruous energies, installing
themselves in that which he considers his "I", form
there a swarming throng.

This actually includes a considerable number of
beings belonging to what we call the Past.

To a Westerner, Plato, Zeno, Jesus, Saint Paul,
Calvin, Diderot, Jean Jacques Rousseau, Christopher
Columbus, Marco Polo, Napoleon, and many others
may constitute a diversified crowd, turbulent and

quarrelsome, of which each member, thirsting for pre-eminence, tries to impose the repetition of his own physical and mental movements and, with that object, pulls in different directions the strings which move the poor "I", too blind to make out these phantoms and powerless to put them in their place.

I have quoted some names taken by chance as being those of personalities with which a Westerner might have been in contact in the course of his reading and during his education. These names are only examples. The guests, whom X shelters in his particular guest-house, are not at all the same as those who live with Y.

The influences which act on an Indian or a Chinese, evidently emanate from people of their respective races or those who have been concerned in the history of their countries.

*

* *

When the student becomes aware of this crowd in himself, he should avoid imagining, as some do, that it represents memories of his preceding lives. There is no lack of those who state and are convinced that such and such a personage, who lived in the past, is reincarnated in them.[11] Stories depicting reincarna-

---

[11] Such a belief is not peculiar to Asiatics. It is also to be found among certain Westerners. An amusing point to note on this subject

tions are innumerable in Asia where they keep alive the childish thirst for the marvellous among the masses.

According to the Secret Teachings, the "crowd of others" is made up of quite different things than "memories". It is formed by living beings whose activity follows its course and will continue it indefinitely while taking various shapes for *there is no death*.

It is not the "memory" of Plato or of Jesus which exists in Mr. Peter or in Mr. Smith. There are Plato and Jesus themselves, ever-living and active thanks to the energies which they have formerly set in motion. And the men who bore these names were themselves only the manifestation of multiple energies. In Plato teaching in Greece, in Jesus moving about in Galilee, just as in Mr. Peter or in Mr. Smith, were a crowd of living presences whose ancestry is lost in the unfathomable depths of eternity.

Does that mean that the various personalities who, together, form an *Ego* remain inert or, in other

---

is that the person "reincarnated" generally boasts of having been, in his preceding lives, an important personality, or even several such in succession. No one seems to remember having been an obscure cobbler or a humble farm labourer. At least one does not hear of such.

words, does it mean that this *Ego* is in no way active?
—In no way, is the answer in the Secret Teachings.
The individual Peter or Smith is a centre of energies
which, at each of his gestures, each of his words, each
of his thoughts, shoots out into the world and there
produces effects. It is not only famous persons as
Plato, Jesus, or the Buddha, who are found in the
assemblies which constitute the individuals, our contemporaries; it is also the obscure cobblers, the
humble farm-workers who no one seems inclined to
claim as having been "himself" during his former
lives.

Everyone, big and little, strong and weak, works
continually—and in general unconsciously—at the
formation of new groups whose members, through
lack of perspicacity, are not aware of their hetero-
geneity and, who insensible to the discordance of
their voices, or without dwelling on it, shout in
chorus "I", I am Me!

Such are in general, the theories concerning the
multiplicity and the succession of lives considered as
individual, which are set forth in the Secret
Teachings.

It is well to add that the forces assembled in the
shape of Peter or that of Smith are not equal in power.
There are some which take a dominant position and

relegate their companions in the background, or even suppress them.[12]

It is to these predominating forces that the Tibetan Masters of the reserved teachings appeal to explain in an elevated manner which is strictly in agreement with the doctrine of the non-existence of the homogeneous and permanent *ego*, the phenomenon of the *tulkus*[13] which is very much in evidence in their country.

We know that the *tulkus* are those individuals whom foreigners very incorrectly call "Living Buddhas". In fact the *tulku* is considered as being the reincarnation of a former individual, this latter having himself been the reincarnation of another previous individual, and so on, forming a series of reincarnations which goes back, in the past, to a personality more or less eminent who may have lived several centuries before.

It is clear that this conception implies the belief in an *"ego"* which is permanent and which transmigrates like a man changing house, which is the Hindu point of view. Buddhism, however, categorically denies the existence of the *ego*. The generality

---

[12] On this point see in the appendices of my book "Buddhism, its doctrines and methods" a Tibetan parable concerning *the person*".

[13] Spelling *sprul sku*. On the subject of *tulkus* see my book: "Mystics and Magicians of Tibet", page 109.

of Buddhists automatically repeat the classic formula of this denial, like the faithful of all religions reciting their respective creeds without understanding the meaning of the words they recite, but, practically, the majority of Buddhists see in these successive lives the travels of a wandering entity.

I have just stated that those initiated in the Secret Teachings see this question otherwise.

Among the forces combined into the form of an individual one of them, or several of them together, may aim at a goal which cannot be attained in the short period of time of one human life. A strong determination to create an instrument able to continue the efforts which will be interrupted by death can, it is said, succeed in giving rise to the birth of an individual who will become this instrument, or can possess itself of an already existing individual and guide his activity in a suitable direction to lead to the desired result.

Such is the theory. The name *tulku* agrees perfectly. *Tulku* literally means an "illusory body" created by magic.[14] There is thus no permanent *ego* which transmigrates.

_____

[14] The Tibetans distinguish between *tulkus* and *tulpas*. The *tulkus* are men and women, apparently living normal lives like our own. *Tulpas* are more or less ephemeral creations which may take different forms: man, animal, tree, rock, etc., at the will of the magician who,

What is it that in the Secret Teachings is said about the fourth of the supernormal powers, that which allows the knowledge of preceding lives? This is sometimes expressed picturesquely as knowing one's preceding dwellings, a way of putting it which is very likely to give a wrong understanding of the subject.

The reader has already seen from what has been said above, that the initiate in the Secret Teachings considers *his* preceding lives as being manifold. Not only manifold in succession which extends in time, but manifold in various directions, in coexistent episodes, in separate rays emanating from numerous clusters of forces—clusters which we call *individuals*.

It follows that if Plato, Jesus and others continue their lives in numbers of Peters and Smiths, each of these Peters and Smiths is in no way authorized to believe himself Plato, or Jesus, or any other reincarnated. Only a fraction of these personalities re-live in him. It has there taken the form of tendencies,

---

created them, and behave like the being whose form they happen to have. These *tulpas* coexist with their creator and can be seen simultaneously with him. In some cases they may survive him, or, during his life, free themselves from his domination and attain a certain independence. The *tulku*, on the contrary, is the incarnation of a lasting energy directed by an individual with the object of continuing a given kind of activity after his death. The *tulku* does not coexist with his ancestor.

of sentiments transmitted by means of reading, or speeches having called up the thoughts, the words or the deeds of these eminent individuals. But, once more, let me repeat that the hearing of the words and the sight of the actions of common performers, the cobbler, the servant, etc., can have brought to Peter or Smith even during the life of this cobbler or servant, elements which have taken root, which are incarnated in him, and have determined certain of the mental or physical activities of Peter or Smith. That is to say, have lived in them.

This fragmentation of causes and energies is to be remembered when one tries to investigate one's "ancient dwellings".

To recall them is to review the various persons living in us, to examine them, questioning them insistently, showing up their habitual lies, removing the mask from those who try to assume a false identity and, above all, in not trying to deceive one-self concerning the quality and the moral value, the intellectual and social worth of the guests whom one harbours or, more accurately, who have been *us* in the past and continue to be *us* in the present.

CHAPTER VII

"All the magnificence of kings and of their ministers, appear to the eyes of a Buddha, as so much spittle and dust.

"To his eyes gold, silver and all treasures look merely like pebbles."

—(Sūtra in 42 articles)[1]

"As images seen in a dream, thus should one see all things."

—(Vajracchedikā sūtra of the Prajñā pāramitā)[2]

Two points of view, two mental attitudes. The Sūtra in 42 articles reflects the state of mind of him who has understood the vanity and even the distasteful character of anything which the masses consider desirable. It is the attitude of the man who, as an

---

[1] The Sūtra in 42 articles was carried from India to China about the year 65 of the Christian era. There are translations of it in Chinese, Tibetan, Manchu and Mongol. It is thought to be the first Buddhist work which has been translated into Chinese.

[2] Vajracchedikā, in Tibetan: *Dordji tchöd pa* (rdé rjé gchod pa) which means "the Cutting Diamond". This word "diamond" is understood in the Sacred Literature as meaning that which is most 'excellent". The Sūtra is thought to lead those who study it to Knowledge which cuts, breaks the bonds due to error, especially the belief in the *ego*, and to produce spiritual illumination.

effect of semi-clairvoyance, turns away from the world with scorn and disgust.

The other attitude is that of the calm thinker whose judgment has penetrated deeper into the nature of the manifestations by which the world is made perceptible to us. He does not turn away. He feels neither scorn nor disgust. "Splendour of kings, riches" are not seen by him as spittle and pebbles . . . . He sees them *void*.

The meaning of the term *void* which we have already employed and to which we shall recur in what follows, has been the subject of numerous commentaries and eager controversies among Buddhist philosophers. Westerners who have understood it are rare. Although understood differently by the Theravādins (Hīnayānists) and by the Doctors of the Mahāyāna, neither the ones nor the others have ever thought of making the void of which they speak an equivalent of nothingness.

Nothingness is one of those words which one uses without trying to form a clear idea of what it can mean. Absolute Nothing is inconceivable. He who says "Nothing" incorporates himself in this vacuity simply by the fact that he himself must exist in order to have the idea of it.

We have already seen in the preceding chapters that void means empty in its own nature, devoid of a "self" distinct and independent from the elements which compose it, which render it perceptible, active, efficient.

It has been explained that that which is "compound", which is constituted by the combination of elements as a house is made up of stones, wood, etc., is only a collection, a group and in no way a real "ego". Thus the individual is empty, everything is empty, because one can find nothing in it except the parts which constitute it.

It is especially in this way that the Theras of the Southern School (Theravāda) explain the meaning of the word "void" as used by them.

Among the Mahāyānists, "void" has the meaning of "relative". All that which exists does so in relation to something else, is based on something else and only exists because of this relationship. Because of this relationship which is the indispensable basis of their existence, individuals, as well as all things, are void of self essence. They are products due to the conjunction and co-existence of causes: they are neither autogenous nor autonomous, and consequently they are only names denoting somethings which is void of intrinsic reality.

The two explanations tend to show the same fact: they are brought together in the Secret Teachings.

When the student has understood the meaning of them he is directed to examine another meaning of the Void, that which, in the works of the Mahāyānist philosophers, gives the Void as the origin of all things.

In this sense the Tibetans metaphorically call the Void *ka dag,* an abbreviation of *ka nes dag pa* which means pure from its origin, or *ji* (gzhi) *ka dag*: fundamental purity. In its proper sense the Void is called *tong pa gnid* (stong pa ñid).

The adjective "pure" is not understood here in the moral sense which we sometimes give it: it means "unmixed", excluding all other elements.

Void is understood as a state in which the elements do not produce any combination, give rise to no phenomenon, a state in which only forces, latent and non-manifest, exist. Being the sphere of complete absence of manifestation, the Void is inconceivable.

It should be noted that in the Secret Teachings the expression "Origin of things" is not applied to a beginning of the Universe, like that which is depicted in various ways by the different religions and philosophic doctrines in their metaphysical treatises.

According to the Secret Teachings the origin of things is not situated in any place or moment of past time ; it is produced now, at each instant, in our minds. At every moment the subjective image which is the world, arises in our mind only to sink back and dissolve in it the moment after, like the "waves which arise from the sea and fall back into it".[3]

This root originally free from any admixture, origin of the illusory world in which we live, is a fleeting contact with some unknowable instant of Reality, some indefinable force which the *vāsanās* obscure at once, superimposing on it the screen on which the images which we see, are painted.[4]

*

*   *

Eighteen kinds of Void[5] are enumerated in Buddhist Philosophy, illustrating what has just been said, that the Absolute, the Reality, are void of all our conceptions.

*

*   *

---

[3] A frequent comparison in the works of Indian philosophies.

[4] See Chapter II, page 21.

[5] Interior Void. External Void. Internal and external Void. Void of Void. Great Void. Real Void. Compound Void. Non-compound Void. Unlimited Void. Void without beginning, nor end. Void which rejects nothing. Intrinsic Void. Void of all elements. Void of any character of its own. Void of perceptions, of representations. Void of proprieties. Void of its own essence. Void without any properties.

These last three kinds are also qualified as: Void of existence, Void of non-existence. Void at the same time of being and non-being. Denial and affirmation of a thing co-existing with its opposite are usual in the Buddhist philosophical phraseology; it is a way of expressing the fact that the mind comes upon the unconceivable.

Thus we have indirectly returned to the co-existence of two worlds which are indissolubly united: the world of Reality and the relative world which has been mentioned above. A third world, the imaginary one, is added to these two in the Secret Teachings. It is true to say that this last is mentioned by Mahāyānist authors, but they mostly consider it completely unreal while, in the Secret Teachings, it is admitted to have a certain degree of reality.

What is the imaginary world?—It has been variously defined as the realm of pure phantasy, of subjective visions, of ideas which are baseless or which seem to arise without any cause. These are "flowers in the sky" according to the picturesque and classical expression in Indian philosophy.

The Secret Teachings object to this definition on the grounds that nothing can occur without a cause and that disorderly imaginings have bases which can easily be discovered in the relative world.

If one imagines a green dog with an elephant's trunk, the component parts of this fantastic animal have been supplied by the memory of objects which our sense have shown us. We have seen dogs, seen elephants with their trunks, and seen the colour green.

It is the same with pictures seen in dreams which are equally based on those which we are accustomed

to see when awake. Again it is the same with ideas
and feelings which arise in us during sleep for they
too have their roots in our mentality, either in the
conscious part of it, or in the subconscious.

From these different facts the Secret Teachings
conclude that the imaginanry world is not wholly
unreal, that it is close to the relative world and intermingled with it.

*
*   *

The Tibetan doubtobs[6] are considered to be ex-
perts in the art of creating tulpas,[7] imaginary forms
which are a sort of robots which they control as they
wish, but which, sometimes, manage to acquire some
kind of autonomous personality.

It is also stated that during their periods of deep
meditation the doubtobs surround themselves with
an impassable occult protective zone which guarantees
their complete isolation, this zone extending at times
right round their hermitage, when they adopt the
life of an anchorite.

---

[6] Doubtob (grubthob) means he who has "succeeded", who has
"accomplished"; this implies. who has acquired supernormal powers.
These are they who are called siddha in Sanskrit.

[7] The belief in tulpas is universal in Tibet and there are many
stories about them, some of these stories being terribly tragic. For
more details about tulpas see my books "Mystics and Magicians of
Tibet", "Initiations lamaïques" and "La Vie surhumaine de Guésar
de Ling" (the Tibetan Iliad).

Novices who are training themselves according
to the methods of the Secret Teachings, are sometimes advised to exercise themselves in creating
mentally around themselves an environment completely different from that which is considered real.
For example, seated in their room, they conjure up
a forest. If the exercise is successful they will no
longer be conscious of the objects around them which
will have given place to trees, copses, and they will
travel through the forest feeling all the sensations
usual to those who move in the woods.

The usefulness of such exercises is to lead the
novice to understand the superficial nature of our
sensations and perceptions, since they can be caused
by things which we consider unreal.

According to the Secret Teachings in denying
them any reality, we may perhaps be wrong, for any
mental creation possesses a kind of reality which is
peculiar to it since it can show itself effective.

*

*   *

The relative world is close to the imaginary
world because, as has been said, error and illusion
dominate it. That which appears to us as round
may, in fact, be square, and so on. Most of humanity
are unconscious of the fact that they live and move
in a world of phantasmagoria ; however, some have

perceived this and have discovered in themselves the origin of this phantasmagoria. Is this to say that, from that moment, they have entirely freed themselves from it?—Not always. Perhaps one ought to say: not often. They remain in the position of those sleepers who, although conscious of the fact that they are dreaming, continue to dream and even follow with interest the adventures of their dreams.[8] But the scenes which they meet no longer affect them. Perceptions and sensations leave them unmoved, glide off them without arousing desire or repulsion.[9] In the words of the Buddhist texts, all the agitation of this world of relativity and illusion only produces in them this appreciation: "This is only that!"[10]

To say "This is only that!" does not mean that "*that*" does not exist. To state that the world in which we live has no existence whatever would be, on our part, an absurdity. Such a declaration would be equivalent of saying that we do not exist, for, such *as we are*, we belong to the world of relativity, our existence is dependent on such a world and, outside of it, we do not exist.

However in the same way as this world, we are

---

[8] This is quite a usual thing among most of those who have practised the Yoga exercises with this object.

[9] "As water slips off a lotus leaf or a grain of mustard from the point of a needle" (Dhammapada 401).

[10] Dīgha Nikāya.

only "*that*". The vanity of man jibs at that statement which is, all the same, indisputable. Man is accustomed to think himself important, he takes pleasure in this flattering idea, he has invented doctrines to give himself a central place in the universe, even going so far as to declare that the whole universe with its myriads of worlds, was constructed solely for him. His "*Ego*", he likes to think, holds the attention of super-human Powers ; Gods and Demons carefully watch his acts and thoughts, applauding some and punishing others. In himself man has built a sub-office of the invisible tribunal of divine judges, and there he distributes praises and blame ; from the decrees he issues, there follow the vainglorious satisfaction caused by deeds which are called "virtuous" and the tragic dramas of remorse springing from acts considered wrong or sinful.

When Nietzsche gave out his dramatic proclamation concerning that which is beyond Good or Evil, his vehemence sprang from the belief which he still held in the existence of Good and Evil in the common acceptation of the words, and also from his persistent faith in the importance of man and of his acts. An adept of the Secret Teachings would have smiled on hearing him, for all grandiloquence is banished from these teachings. In them the pupil is coldly told : "Learn that thou art only *void* and

that thy deeds are in no way *thine,* but the simple
work of energies forming ephemeral combinations by
the effect of manifold causes among which a piercing
and trained sight (*lhag thong*) discovers the most
direct, while the innumerable others remain undis-
coverable in the depths of time and space, in the
depths of "memories" (vāsanā) without any knowable
beginning. Thus thou hast no reason to be either
proud or humiliated. Realise thine own insigni-
ficance."

The fact of having realised an accurate idea of
the unimportant place which one occupies even in
the relative world, does not necessarily lead to remaining inert, overwhelmed by the proofs of one's
littleness. Action is in no way excluded.

The student who has succeeded in understanding
that his life is a dream which he himself supplies
with agreeable or terrifying scenes, can ensure that
the dream does not become a nightmare. He can
strive to furnish this relative world, his own creation,
with things likely to lead to his own wellbeing, his
happiness. Illusory objects, pictures like those offered
by mirages, are nevertheless, efficient, that is to say,
real for the dreamer, made of the same substance as
they are and sharing with them the same degree of
illusory existence.

On the other hand, the well-informed dreamer

may cease taking pleasure in dreaming. He may stop imitating those dreamers who, enjoying the phantasmagoria which they watch and in which they play a part, persist in wishing to remain asleep. In truth, why do the dreamers fear awakening, why do they imagine in advance other dreams of hells and heavens which await them after death? It is because they fear that with the disappearance of the "images seen in dreams", the illusory *"Ego"* which is an integral part of them will disappear. They have not yet perceived that the real face of this chimerical *"Ego"* is the face of Death. As long as the idea of this impermanent *Ego* lasts, this simple mass of elements which various causes have brought together and which other causes will separate, death also subsists. The Dhammapada alludes to the disappearance of this phantom from the field of our mental activity when it refers to whom "death does not see", that is, he for whom death does not exist.

The awakening is liberation, salvation. The Secret Teachings propose no other object than this to their pupils.

To wake up... The Buddhas have done nothing else than this, and it is this awakening which has made them become Buddhas.

*

*   *

Some people may ask: how will the awakened one, in his new state of "Awakened One", act towards others?

The reply to this question is: Do *others* really exist?—Are not *others* like the other objects which furnish our environment, just projections of our thought, and considering that our senses deceive us in everything, should we accept their evidence when they set before us the form of *another* wholly distinct from ourselves?

In any case it is impossible for us, who are not awakened, to form an idea of the condition in which an *"Awakened One"* finds himself. It is similar to the impossibility for a sleeper, absorbed in his dream, to be aware of what exists outside the dream.

From a practical point of view, we find inducements to action such as that contained in the *Vajracchedikā Sūtra*:

"It is when one no longer believes in the 'I', in the 'person', when one has rejected all beliefs, that the time has come to distribute gifts."

The Masters of the Secret Teachings give this text and others like it to their pupils as subjects of meditation. Their enigmatic character weakens and disappears little by little in the course of prolonged meditations and they throw a clear light on the path of the pilgrim making his way through the relative world, marching towards the farthest conceptions of his mind: a world of Reality, a world of the Void.

The question of *Nirvāna* naturally arises here, for *Nirvāna* is, according to general opinion among Buddhists, the opposite of the world of impermanence: of the *samsāra*.

This opinion is examined and disputed in the Oral Secret Teachings. It is said there, that it is tinged by the idea of the "I" and of the "other", by ideas of separate places occupying distinct areas in space, all such conceptions being rejected in these teachings.

Nirvāna and *samsāra*, we are told, are not two different things, but one and the same thing seen from two different points of view by onlookers whose degree of sharpness of mental vision differs widely. The ignorant man, whose "mental eye is covered with a thick layer of dust"[11] sees the painful round of deaths and successive births with all that they imply of trouble and suffering. The Sage, whose "mental eye has been freed from all dust" which could interfere with its penetrating vision, he, by means of *lhag thong* (transcendent insight) can contemplate *nirvāna*.

---

[11] Mahāvagga. See Chapter I.

The awakening from the dream in which we are involved and which we continue to live even while being more or less clearly conscious that we dream, will this awakening lead us to another world? Will it not rather consist in the perception of the underlying reality in the world in which we find ourselves? Ought we not therefore to understand that *Nirvāna* and *samsāra,* as reality and relativity, are fancies created by our mind, attributing them to the unknowable?

It is stated in the great work of Nāgārjuna, the Prajñā Pāramitā, in writing about the Void, this synonym of Reality:

"Form is the Void and the Void is the form. The Void is nothing else than form and form is nothing else than the Void. Outside the Void there is no form, and outside the form there is no Void."

The same declaration is repeated about the other elements composing the individual, perceptions, sensations, mental activity, consciousness. It is, again, repeated concerning all the points of Buddhist Doctrine, about the Buddha himself, about everything. Everything which we call "ourselves" and the furnishings of things and phenomena which make up our environment, whether physical or psychical, the "world", all that *is* the Void and the Void *is* all that. Outside of that there is no Void, and outside of the Void nothing of all that exists.

Thus the world of relativity is not a limited sphere separated by a rigid frontier from the real world. Nowhere does there exist a line of demarcation, for everywhere there is interpenetration.

The world of relativity is the Void-Reality and the Void-Reality is the relative world. Outside of this latter there is no Void-Reality, and outside the Void-Reality there is no relative world.

Will the student, at this point, think that he has attained to Truth? Will he stop there?—His Master will strongly dissuade him. If he stops, he will only have struck an obstacle which will immobilize him. To *believe* that one *knows* is the greatest of the barriers which prevent *knowledge*. To imagine that one possesses absolute certainty begets a fatal mental stagnation.

The attitude which these Teachings advocate is one of a strong will to know all that it is possible to know, never to halt on the road to investigation which extends infinitely far before the feet of the explorer.

The pupil may be somewhat bewildered at having seen ideas considered as most solidly based, first shaken and then overthrown around him, so the

Master will suggest that to see in everything nothing but illusion may also be an illusion which must be put aside in passing and, he will willingly end his lessons with these words: "I have never intended to teach you something, but only to incite you to think, to doubt, to seek."

*

*   *

The subject of the Oral Teachings which are called secret and given out by Masters belonging to different Schools of Philosophy in Tibet is far from being fully covered here. It includes numerous original interpretations of the theories laid down by the Doctors of the Hīnayāna and of the Mahāyāna. My "account" is limited to pointing out the main lines of these Teachings and the spirit which infuses them. To what extent I have succeeded in giving a clear enough idea is something which I cannot judge ; only my readers can say.

In any case it seems to me fit and proper to finish with the declaration which is habitual with oriental authors when explaining a doctrine:

If my readers find unintelligibility and mistakes in my account, the fault is mine who have not been able to express, as they ought to have been, the Teachings which were communicated to me.

APPENDIX

According to an ancient tradition, King Srong bstan Gampo (VIIIth century), the most famous of the kings of Tibet, explained to a group of selected listeners the deep meaning of the doctrine of the Void.

He said:

"Although the Buddha stated categorically that he had set out the whole of His Teachings without hiding anything or holding back any part thereof so as to form an esoteric section, the various degrees of intelligence among his hearers, and, even more, the different degrees of understanding of those who, after Him, continued to spread His Doctrine, have necessarily brought about divisions among those who profess to be His disciples. None of them has thought of rejecting the fundamental principles of the Master's Teaching: the deviations have taken place as to the greater or lesser importance to be given to such and such of them, or to the way in which these fundamental principles should be understood. Thus it happened that particular developments and a deeper way of understanding the fundamental data of the original doctrine have occasioned a series of teachings considered as beyond the reach of less-developed intelligences, and which the Masters, who thought themselves in possession of the key to them, considered should only be taught to those disciples fit to understand them.[1]

Srong bstan Gampo appears in history as a clever and daring chief. King of Lhasa, he showed himself powerful

---

[1] See what has been already said on this point.

enough to overawe the Chinese Emperor Tai Tsun and force him, despite the repugnance which the latter felt at allying himself with a "Barbarian", to send him, as wife, one of his daughters, the Princess Wen Tchen.[2]

However, in the memory of the Tibetans, he who is honoured is not the mighty sovereign, but a Srong bstan Gampo who was super-human and endowed with a mythological biography.

According to this biography, Srong bstan Gampo was much more than a great initiate. He possessed, innately, the deep understanding of the highest Knowledge owing to his being an avatar of the sublime and compassionate Chenrezigs,[3] patron of Tibet, who had incarnated so as to teach and guide his chosen children: the good people of the Land of Snows.

The sermons attributed to Srong bstan Gampo extend over various stages of understanding of the Buddhist Doctrine, and reach their highest point in that one which concerns the theory of the Void.

Void, we have already said, does not mean "nothingness". On the other hand, this term does not belong to a cosmogenic system beginning with a declaration analogous to "In the beginning was the Void".[4]

Nevertheless, some people have thought to find an explanation of the origin of the Universe in the classic state-

---

[3] Chenrezigs is the Tibetan name of Avalokiteshvara.

[2] The marriage took place in 641.

[4] It is well-known that the Buddhist Doctrine excludes any kind of cosmological system, any description of a beginning, in the absolute sense, of the Universe.

ment *"Ji ka dag . . . Tsal len dup"*[5] which means "In the
originally pure base, an energy arose by itself".

The Secret Teachings expounded in the sayings attributed to Srong bstan Gampo contradict this opinion.
According to them, the original Void (*ji ka dag*) is the
inconceivable form of the Mind existing before an autogenous energy (*tsal len dup*) caused the *saṁskāras* (mental
composition) to arise in it, creators of the images which
constiute our world. It is in this void of the mind, comparable to the special void, that are born, act and disappear
all the phenomena perceived by our senses, phenomena
which we wrongly imagine to be scenes unfolding outside
ourselves, whereas they only exist in us.

During the king's sermons the eighteen sorts of void
listed in philosophic works are explained in relation with
the Void of the original mind. On the whole we are told:

"The mind is comparable with space ; like space it has
neither interior nor exterior ; in its depths one finds nothing
but the Void.

"Ideas of continuity or discontinuity cannot be applied
to the mind ; it escapes them, just as in the case of space one
cannot conceive it either as limited or as infinite.

"It is impossible to discover a place where the mind is
born, a place where it dwells afterwards, a place where it
ceases to exist. Like space, the mind is void in the three
times: past, present and future.

"In space we see clouds arise and vanish, without being
able to find a dwelling for them from where they emerge

---

[5] Spelling *Gzi ka dag—rtsal len grub*. This declaration is
especially honoured by the Sect of the "Great Accomplishment"
(Dzogs chen pa).

and to where they can go back to. In space we see the sun
shine, the moon, the stars, the planets, but what is space
itself?

"The essence of space, its very nature, space *in itself*,
are beyond all words, all imagination. It is the same with
the original mind, void of any essence or any qualities of
its own: impossible to grasp."

The "beyond" is also explained in relation with the
Void. "To go beyond Knowledge" means to immerse the
mind once more in its original virgin world which, like space,
can contain all because it is void.

As a conclusion to these dissertations we can say, that
the worthlessness of the doctrines and methods, which claim
to elevate us above our world of relativity, is clearly
denounced. Our world is limited, but its limits are not
perceptible to us and, on our scale, it is practically unlimited.

The more compactly we furnish it with the help of
theories, opinions, imaginations, the more all these, acting
as bonds, tie us down and keep us prisoners.

The "going beyond", the "non-activity" are the means
for us to attain mental freedom. In truth we have nothing
to *do*, it is a question of *"undoing"*, of clearing the ground
of our mind, of making it, as much as possible, clean, void.
The Void is, here, for us always a synonym of liberation.